gets you through

CW00540437

EDEXCEL GCSE 9-1
MATHS
HIGHER
PRACTICE TEST PAPERS

GCSE

MIKE FAWCETT

Contents

ACKNOWLEDGEMENTS

The author and publisher are grateful to the copyright holders for permission to use quoted materials and images.

Calculator image © Shutterstock.com/Bryan Solomon

Every effort has been made to trace copyright holders and obtain their permission for the use of copyright material. The author and publisher will gladly receive information enabling them to rectify any error or omission in subsequent editions. All facts are correct at time of going to press.

Published by Letts Educational
An imprint of HarperCollins*Publishers*
1 London Bridge Street
London SE1 9GF

ISBN: 9780008276126

First published 2018

10 9 8 7 6 5 4 3

© HarperCollins*Publishers* Limited 2018

All rights reserved. No part of this publication may be reproduced, stored in a retrieval system, or transmitted, in any form or by any means, electronic, mechanical, photocopying, recording or otherwise, without the prior permission of Letts Educational.

British Library Cataloguing in Publication Data.

A CIP record of this book is available from the British Library.

Commissioning Editor: Clare Souza
Author: Mike Fawcett
Project Management: Richard Toms
Cover Design: Amparo Barrera
Inside Concept Design: Ian Wrigley
Text Design and Layout: QBS Learning
Production: Natalia Rebow
Printed and bound by CPI Group (UK) Ltd, Croydon, CR0 4YY

GCSE
Mathematics
Higher tier

H

Paper 1 (Non-Calculator)

Time: 1 hour 30 minutes

You must have: Ruler, protractor, pair of compasses, pen, HB pencil, eraser.

Instructions

- Use **black** ink or black ball-point pen. Draw diagrams in pencil.
- Diagrams are **NOT** accurately drawn, unless otherwise indicated.
- Answer **all** questions.
- Answer the questions in the space provided.
- **Calculators may not be used**.
- You must **show all your working out**. Use a separate sheet of paper if needed.

Information

- The total mark for this paper is 80.
- The marks for **each** question are shown in brackets. Use this as a guide as to how much time to spend on each question.

Advice

- Read each question carefully before you start to answer it.
- Keep an eye on the time.
- Try to answer every question.
- Check your answers if you have time at the end.

1   Work out the following. Write your answer as a mixed number if appropriate.

(a) $\frac{3}{5} + \frac{2}{7}$ (2)

....

(b) $\frac{3}{4} \div \frac{2}{3}$ (3)

....

2   Simplify $(x^3)^4$ (1)

....

3   Charlotte, Clarisse and Mathilda share some money in the ratio 4 : 6 : 11

Mathilda receives £200 more than Clarisse.

How much do they each receive?   (3)

Ch : Cl : m
4 : 6 : 11 = 21

Charlotte £..

Clarisse £..

Mathilda £..

4   *AE*, *BF* and *DCG* are parallel.

BC = *CD*

ADB = 22°

EAB = 68°

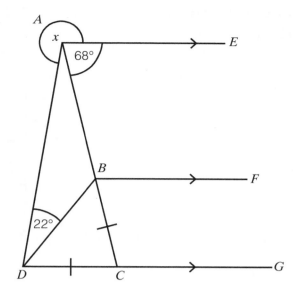

Work out the size of the angle marked *x*. You must show your working. **(4)**

....°

5   Tim and Amanda want to investigate the probability that it will rain on any given day in October.

Tim records the number of days that it rains in a week. Amanda records the number of days that it rains in the whole month.

Here are their results:

	Number of days it rains	Number of days without rain
Tim's results	2	5
Amanda's results	11	20

(a) Write down two different estimates for the probability that it will rain on any given day in October. **(2)**

....

(b) Which is the most reliable estimate from your answers in part (a)? Give a reason for your answer. **(1)**

....

....

....

6   The table shows the heights of basketball players in a school league.

Height, h (in cm)	Frequency	
$155 < h \leqslant 160$	5	✓
$160 < h \leqslant 165$	12	✓
$165 < h \leqslant 170$	18	✓
$170 < h \leqslant 175$	20	✓
$175 < h \leqslant 180$	19	✓
$180 < h \leqslant 185$	17	✓
$185 < h \leqslant 190$	15	✓
$190 < h \leqslant 195$	11	✓

117

(a) Write down the modal class interval for the height of the players. **(1)**

$170 < h \leqslant 175$

(b) Find the class interval which contains the median height. **(2)**

7   **(a)** Solve the inequality $7x - 4 \leqslant 7 + 5x$ **(2)**

(b) Show your answer to part (a) on the number line. **(2)**

8   Work out the answer to $(6.1 \times 10^5) + (4.2 \times 10^4)$

Give your answer in standard form. **(2)**

9 Expand and simplify $(2x + 3)(4x - 2)$ **(2)**

[handwritten working] $8x^2 - 4x - 12x + 12x$

$16x^2 - 6$

10 Here is a linear graph.

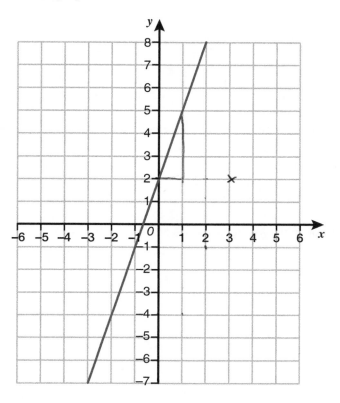

(a) Write down the equation of the line. **(2)**

[handwritten working] $y = mx + c$

$y = mx + 2$

$y = 3x + 2$

(b) Write down the equation of the line which is parallel to the line in part (a) and passes through the point (3, 2). **(2)**

[handwritten working] $y = 3x - 7$

11 A house was bought in 2013.

It was sold in 2017 for £180 000.

The seller made 20% profit.

How much did the seller buy the house for in 2013?

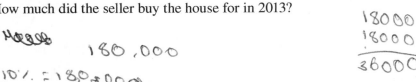

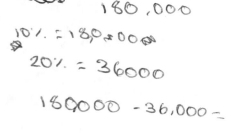

180,000

$10\% = 18,000$

$20\% = 36000$

$180000 - 36,000 =$

£ ....

(2)

12 A construction company pays 15 men to install six kitchens into some new houses.

It will take the 15 men 18 days to complete the kitchens.

Before the work begins, three of the men are called away on another job.

How long will it take the rest of the men to complete the kitchens?

(2)

.... days

13 *BC* is parallel to *DE*.

BC = 4 cm

DE = 10 cm

AD = 7.5 cm

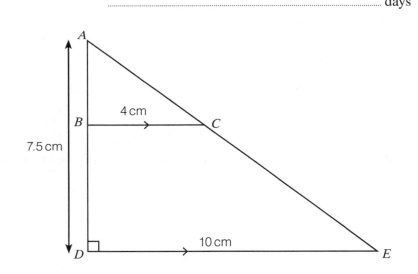

Work out the length of *CE*. **(5)**

.... cm

14   Mr Chan's tutor group has 27 students. They each decide which event they will take part in on sports day.

| 16 choose to do a track event | 6 who choose a track event also choose a field event |

| 4 students decide not to take part |

(a) Show this information on the Venn diagram. **(2)**

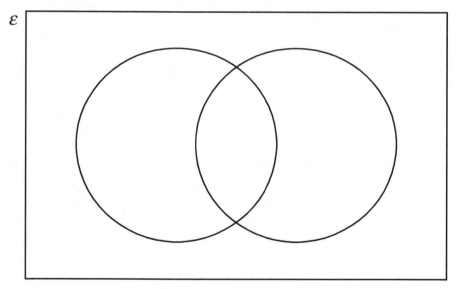

(b) A student is chosen at random from the tutor group.

Find the probability that this student decided to do both a track event and a field event. **(2)**

....

15 Make p the subject of the formula $q = \dfrac{5 + 7p}{p + 1}$ (3)

16 Tim and Andy each did 10 laps of a BMX track and recorded their times.

The box plot shows their results.

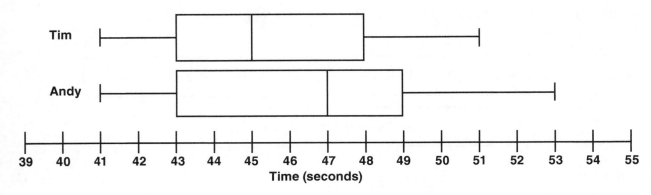

Give two reasons why Tim might be the better rider. (2)

17 Convert $0.3\dot{2}\dot{7}$ to a fraction in its lowest terms. (3)

18 Find the value of $\left(\frac{16}{81}\right)^{-\frac{3}{4}}$

(3)

....

19 The area of this triangle is $1.5\,\text{cm}^2$.

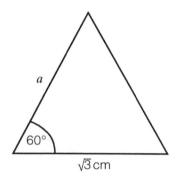

Find the exact value for the length of a.

(4)

$a =$ .... cm

20 (a) Sketch the graph of $y = 3^x$

(2)

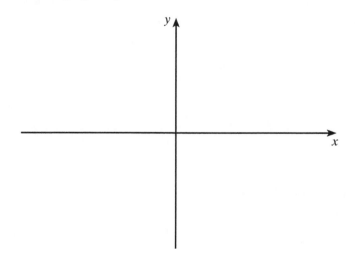

(b)

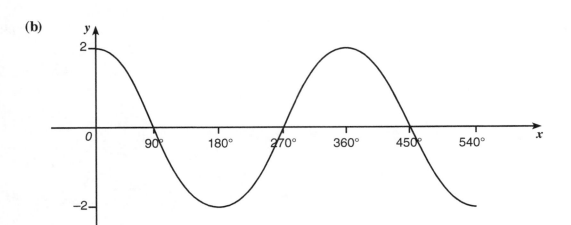

Write down the equation of the graph. **(2)**

....

21 Here is a speed–time graph for a tram journey. The journey took 180 seconds.

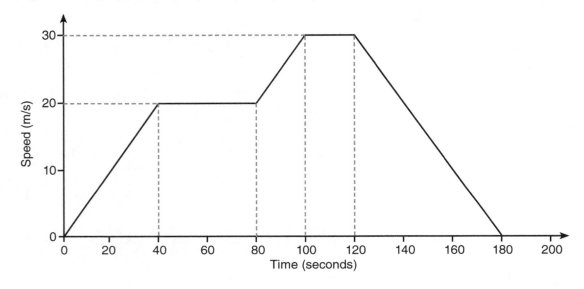

(a) How far did the tram travel in 180 seconds? **(3)**

.... km

(b) Work out the acceleration of the tram for **two** parts of the journey. **(2)**

.... m/s²

22 Express as a single fraction in its simplest form $\dfrac{x+2}{x} - \dfrac{x}{x-1}$

(3)

....

23

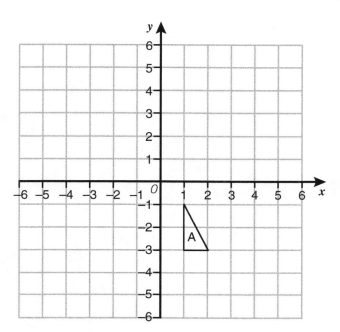

(a) Enlarge shape A by scale factor 2, centre (0, 0) and label the image B.

Rotate shape B 180° clockwise about the origin (0, 0) and label the image C.

(2)

(b) Describe the single transformation which maps shape A on to shape C.

(2)

....

....

24 $f(x) = x^2 + 2$

$g(x) = 3x + 5$

Write fg(x) in the form $ax^2 + bx + c$ **(3)**

....

25 The diagram shows a circle, centre (0, 0).

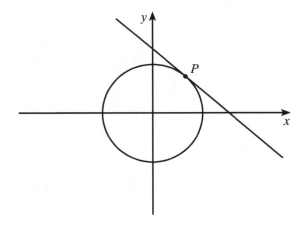

The equation of the tangent to the circle at point P is $y = \dfrac{13 - 2x}{3}$

Write down the coordinates of point P.   **(2)**

(................, ...)

TOTAL FOR PAPER IS 80 MARKS

GCSE
Mathematics

H

Higher tier

Paper 2 (Calculator)

Time: 1 hour 30 minutes

You must have: Ruler, protractor, pair of compasses, pen, HB pencil, eraser, calculator.

Instructions

- Use **black** ink or black ball-point pen. Draw diagrams in pencil.
- Diagrams are **NOT** accurately drawn, unless otherwise indicated.
- Answer **all** questions.
- Answer the questions in the space provided.
- **Calculators may be used**.
- If your calculator does not have a π button, take the value of π to be 3.142 unless the question instructs otherwise.
- You must **show all your working out**. Use a separate sheet of paper if needed.

Information

- The total mark for this paper is 80.
- The marks for **each** question are shown in brackets. Use this as a guide as to how much time to spend on each question.

Advice

- Read each question carefully before you start to answer it.
- Keep an eye on the time.
- Try to answer every question.
- Check your answers if you have time at the end.

1   (a) Factorise fully $12x^2 - 4x$ **(1)**

....

     (b) Simplify $3x^2y^{-1} \times 4xy^3$ **(1)**

....

     (c) Substitute $x = -2$ into the expression $3x^2 - x$ **(1)**

....

2   (a) Use approximation to estimate the answer to $\dfrac{3.9^3}{\sqrt{96.8} - 6.16}$ **(2)**

....

     (b) Use your calculator to find the exact answer to part (a).

     Write down all the figures on your calculator display.   **(1)**

....

     (c) Round your answer in part (b) to 3 significant figures.   **(1)**

....

3   Melanie changes £450 into euros (€) to take on a trip to France.

The exchange rate is £1 = €1.285

(a) Work out how many euros Melanie should get.   (2)

€ ....

Melanie sees a bottle of perfume in France. It costs €36. She knows that the same bottle of perfume costs £27 in England.

(b) What is the difference in price between the two countries? Give your answer in pounds.   (2)

£ ....

4   The expression for the nth term for a sequence of numbers is $\frac{1}{2}(n^2 + n)$.

(a) Work out the 5th and 6th terms in the sequence.   (2)

....

(b) What type of numbers does this sequence generate? You must show your working.   (2)

....

5 Stu is buying tins to make up some food bags for a food bank. Tins of beans are sold in boxes of 14. Tins of soup are sold in boxes of 8.

He wants to buy enough tins of beans and soup so that he can put one of each in each bag.

How many boxes of beans and soup should he buy so that he has none left over? **(3)**

.... boxes of beans

.... boxes of soup

6 Dave is making a concrete mix. He mixes together 500 g of cement, 1 kg of sand and 1.5 kg of water. He makes 2.17 litres of concrete.

Work out the density of the concrete. Give your answer to 2 decimal places. **(2)**

.... g/cm^3

7 Claire, Dionne and Emily are comparing the proportion of boys in each of their Year 9 classes.

Claire says, "In my class, the ratio of boys to girls is 14:13"

Dionne says, "$\frac{5}{9}$ of my class are boys."

Emily says, "46% of my class are girls."

Who has the greatest proportion of boys in their class? You must show your working. **(3)**

....

8   A house was valued at £152 000 in 2015.

The following year the value increased by 2%.

In the two years that followed, the value increased at a rate of 2.5% per year.

(a) How much was the house worth in 2018?   **(3)**

£ ....

(b) If the value of the house continues to increase at a rate of 2.5% per year, in what year will the value of the house exceed £180 000?   **(1)**

....

9   Evaluate the following:

(a) 13^0 **(1)**

....

(b) 2^{-5} **(2)**

....

10 Solve the simultaneous equations

$$3x + 2y = 5$$

$$5x - 7y = 21.25$$

(3)

$x =$ ....

$y =$ ....

11 This steel cone is to be melted down and moulded into the shape of a sphere.

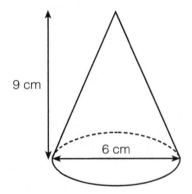

Volume of cone $= \frac{1}{3}\pi r^2 h$

Volume of sphere $= \frac{4}{3}\pi r^3$

9 cm

6 cm

r

Find the radius of the sphere. Give your answer to 3 significant figures.

(4)

.... cm

12 *RST* is a right-angled triangle.

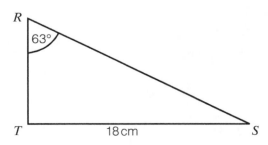

R

63°

T

18 cm

S

Work out the length of *RS*. Give your answer to 1 decimal place. **(3)**

.... cm

13 This cumulative frequency graph shows the distances achieved by 60 shot-put competitors.

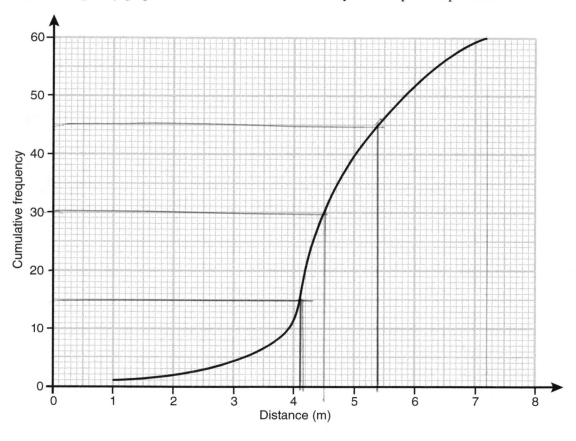

(a) Draw a box plot to display this information. **(3)**

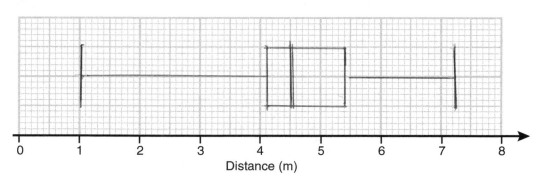

(b) Describe one feature of the box plot. **(1)**

....

....

14 A tile shop sells custom tiles to order. A customer can choose from:

- 5 different sizes
- 12 different designs
- 7 different colours

However, two of the designs are not available for the largest tile size.

Find the total number of different tiles which could be ordered. **(2)**

.... tiles

15 *P, Q, R* and *S* are points on the circumference of a circle.

TU is a tangent to the circle at point *R*.

$PSR = 116°$

$PQ = RQ$

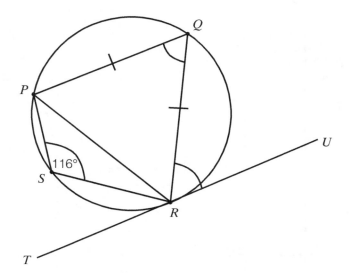

Work out the size of angles *PQR* and *QRU*. Give reasons for your answer.

(a) *PQR* **(2)**

....°

....

(b) *QRU* **(2)**

....°

....

16 x is inversely proportional to the square root of y.

$x = 0.5$ when $y = 25$

Find the value of y when $x = 25$ (3)

$y =$ ....

17 Here are the heights of 50 students in a kick-boxing club.

Construct a histogram to show this information.

Height, h (in cm)	Frequency
$120 < h \leqslant 130$	5
$130 < h \leqslant 140$	7
$140 < h \leqslant 155$	9
$155 < h \leqslant 175$	12
$175 < h \leqslant 185$	11
$185 < h \leqslant 200$	6

(3)

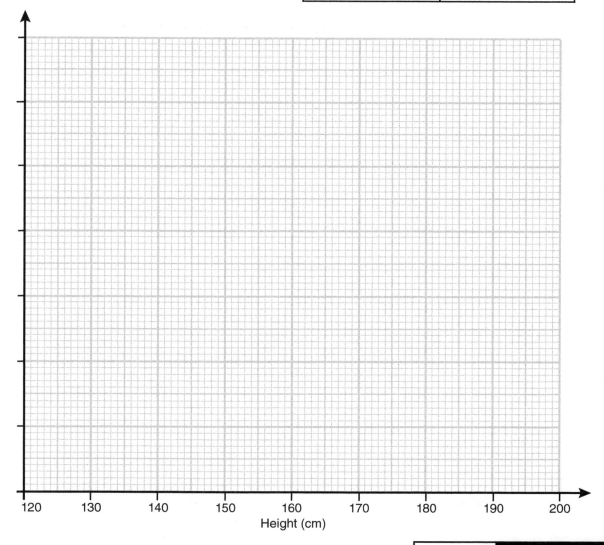

Height (cm)

18 **(a)** Show that the equation $x^3 - 5x + 7 = 0$ can be written as $x = \sqrt[3]{5x - 7}$ **(1)**

(b) Starting with $x_0 = -2$, use the iteration formula $x_{n+1} = \sqrt[3]{5x_n - 7}$ to find the values of x_1 and x_2 **(2)**

$x_1 = $ ....

$x_2 = $ ....

(c) Find the exact value of x correct to 2 decimal places. **(2)**

$x = $ ....

19 **(a)** Prove that the sum of three consecutive odd numbers is always divisible by 3. **(2)**

(b) Prove that the product of three consecutive even numbers is always divisible by 8. (2)

20 Mutiu plants 500 sunflower seeds at the end of August.

If September is warm, then the probability that a seed will survive is 0.9

If September is cold, then the probability that a seed will survive is 0.6

The probability that September will be warm is 0.8

How many of the seeds do you expect will survive? (5)

.... seeds

21 $ABCD$ is a parallelogram.

M is the point on AD where $DM : MA = 1 : 2$

MN is parallel to DB.

$\overrightarrow{DA} = 3\mathbf{a}$

$\overrightarrow{AB} = 5\mathbf{b}$

Work out $\overrightarrow{NC}$ in terms of vectors $\mathbf{a}$ and $\mathbf{b}$. **(4)**

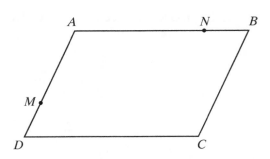

$\overrightarrow{NC} =$ ....

22

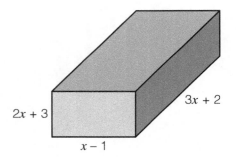

$2x + 3$

$x - 1$

$3x + 2$

Show that the volume of the cuboid can be written in the form $ax^3 + bx^2 + cx + d$ **(3)**

23   The graph of $y = f(x)$ is labelled on the diagram.

(a) Sketch the graph of $y = f(x - 3)$ on the same grid.

(1)

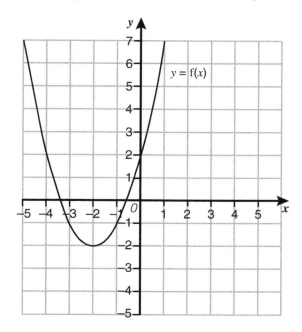

(b) The same graph of $y = f(x)$ is labelled on the diagram.

Another graph is also shown on the grid.

Write down the equation of this graph in terms of $f(x)$.

(2)

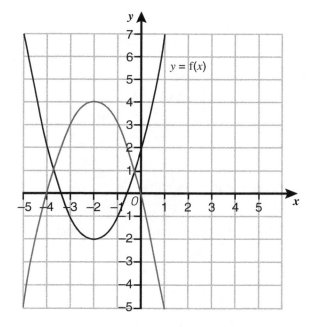

$y =$ ....

TOTAL FOR PAPER IS 80 MARKS

Name: ....

GCSE
Mathematics

H

Higher tier

Paper 3 (Calculator)   Time: 1 hour 30 minutes

You must have: Ruler, protractor, pair
of compasses, pen, HB pencil, eraser,
calculator.

Instructions

- Use **black** ink or black ball-point pen. Draw diagrams in pencil.
- Diagrams are **NOT** accurately drawn, unless otherwise indicated.
- Answer **all** questions.
- Answer the questions in the space provided.
- **Calculators may be used**.
- If your calculator does not have a π button, take the value of π to be
  3.142 unless the question instructs otherwise.
- You must **show all your working out**. Use a separate sheet of paper if needed.

Information

- The total mark for this paper is 80.
- The marks for **each** question are shown in brackets. Use this as a guide
  as to how much time to spend on each question.

Advice

- Read each question carefully before you start to answer it.
- Keep an eye on the time.
- Try to answer every question.
- Check your answers if you have time at the end.

1 What word describes $x^a \times x^b = x^{(a+b)}$?

(1)

....

2 Here are six graphs, A, B, C, D, E and F:

A

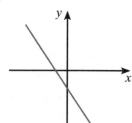

B

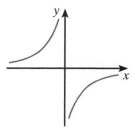

C

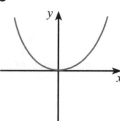

D

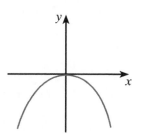

E

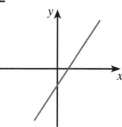

F

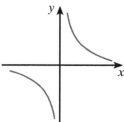

Write down the letter of the graph which matches these equations.

(a) $y = 3x - 2$

.... (1)

(b) $y = x^2$

.... (1)

(c) $y = \frac{1}{x}$

.... (1)

3 John invests £5450 at 3.5% per annum for four years.

Work out the simple interest that he will receive.

(2)

£ ....

4 **(a)** Write 1260 as a product of its prime factors. Give your answer in index form. **(3)**

....

(b) Find the highest common factor (HCF) of 1260 and 1050. **(2)**

....

5 Asif is thinking of a number. He squares his number and then cubes his answer.

Cath says, "You would get the same answer if you raised your original number to the power of 5."

(a) Is Cath correct? Show your working. **(2)**

Asif gets an answer of 1 771 561.

(b) What number was he thinking of? **(1)**

....

6   Carolyn, Del and Julien are playing computer games.

Carolyn has four times as many points as Del.

Del has $\frac{1}{3}$ of the points that Julien has.

Write down the ratio of points that Carolyn, Del and Julien have.   (2)

....

7   The ends of this speedway track are semicircles.

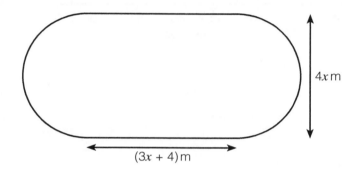

$4x$ m

$(3x + 4)$ m

(a) Write an expression, in terms of x, for the perimeter of the track.   (2)

.... m

The perimeter of the track is 652 m.

(b) Find the value of x. Give your answer correct to 2 decimal places.   (2)

$x =$ ....

8 Tim and Nat have a race.
Tim cycles while Nat runs.

Nat gets a 20-second head start.

They both finish the race at
exactly the same time.

The velocity–time graph shows
the start of the race and it
continues beyond the end of
the race.

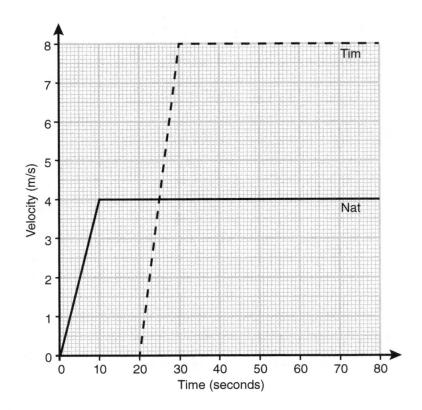

How long was the race in metres? **(4)**

.... m

9 A submarine (S) is marked on the scale diagram. Rocks (R) are also marked on the diagram.

Scale 1 cm : 100 m

R
X

N

S

(a) Find the bearing of the rocks from the submarine. (2)

....°

(b) A sunken galleon is on a bearing of 076° from the submarine at a distance of 500 m.

Mark the position of the galleon (G) on the diagram. (2)

(c) The submarine is going to pass between the rocks and the galleon. It must pass:

- Closer to the galleon than the rocks.
- At least 350 m away from the galleon.

Shade the region through which the submarine can pass. (2)

10 Jill and David are both artists. Here is some information about the price and the number of paintings they sold over a 12-month period.

<table>
<tr><td colspan="2" align="center">**Jill**</td><td></td><td colspan="2" align="center">**David**</td></tr>
</table>

Price, £	Frequency		Price, £	Frequency
$0 < £ \leqslant 100$	3		$0 < £ \leqslant 100$	2
$100 < £ \leqslant 200$	8		$100 < £ \leqslant 200$	4
$200 < £ \leqslant 300$	6		$200 < £ \leqslant 300$	8
$300 < £ \leqslant 400$	7		$300 < £ \leqslant 400$	6

On average, who earned the most money per painting? Show your working. (5)

....

11 The graph of $y = x^2$ is drawn on the grid.

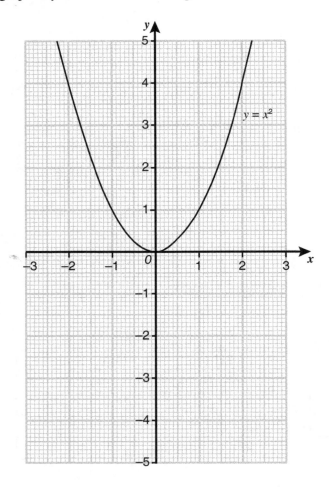

(a) On the grid plot the graph of $y = 1 - x$ **(2)**

(b) Hence, solve the equation $x^2 = 1 - x$

Give your answers to 1 decimal place.   **(2)**

$x =$ .... and $x =$ ....

12 Jason is waiting for a delivery of concrete and a delivery of roof tiles for his building project.

The probability that his concrete will arrive on time is 0.75

The probability that his roof tiles will arrive on time is 0.65

(a) Complete the probability tree diagram. **(2)**

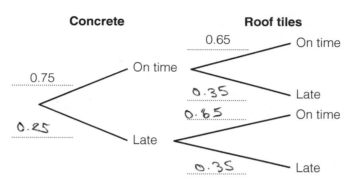

(b) Find the probability that both of the deliveries will arrive late. **(2)**

0.25 × 0.35 = 0.0875

.... 0.0875 ....

13 A council wants to reduce the waste going to landfill sites by 15% per year over the next five years. In 2017, 20 000 tonnes of waste went to landfill sites.

(a) How many tonnes of waste do the council expect to go to landfill sites in 2022? **(2)**

.... tonnes

Konji doesn't think that the council will reach its target. She predicts that there will be 10 000 tonnes of waste going to landfill sites by 2022.

(b) What percentage reduction would this be per year? Give your answer to the nearest 1%. **(3)**

....%

14 Shade the region on the graph which satisfies the following inequalities:

$2y + x > 0$ $\qquad\qquad$ $x < 0$ $\qquad\qquad$ $y \leqslant 2$ $\hfill$ **(3)**

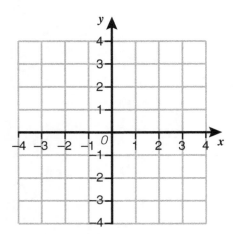

15 The diagram shows a triangle ABC with each of the corners touching the circumference of a circle.

$AB = 10.5\,\text{cm}$

$OC = 6\,\text{cm}$

AC is the diameter of the circle.

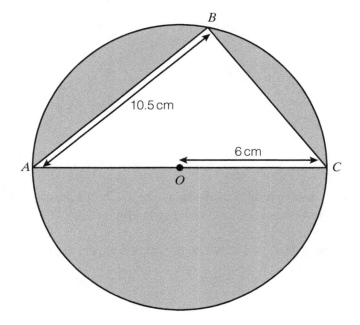

Find the area of the shaded section. $\hfill$ **(5)**

.... cm^2

16 The graph shows the height of water in a container as it is filled over a period of five seconds. The container is being filled at a constant rate.

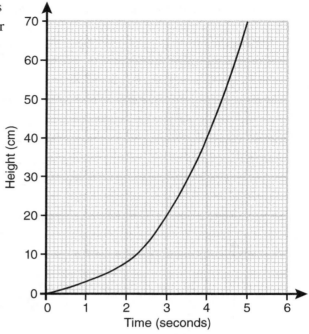

(a) Draw a sketch of the container. **(1)**

(b) Estimate the rate at which the height is increasing at exactly three seconds. **(2)**

.... cm/s

17 Solve the equation $2x^2 + 8x = 3$

Give your answer to 3 decimal places. **(3)**

$x =$ .... and $x =$ ....

18   The table shows the lengths of films released at a cinema in a month.

Length, l (mins)	Frequency
$60 < l \leqslant 80$	4
$80 < l \leqslant 100$	17
$100 < l \leqslant 120$	18
$120 < l \leqslant 140$	13
$140 < l \leqslant 160$	8
$160 < l \leqslant 180$	4

(a) Show this information as a cumulative frequency graph.   (3)

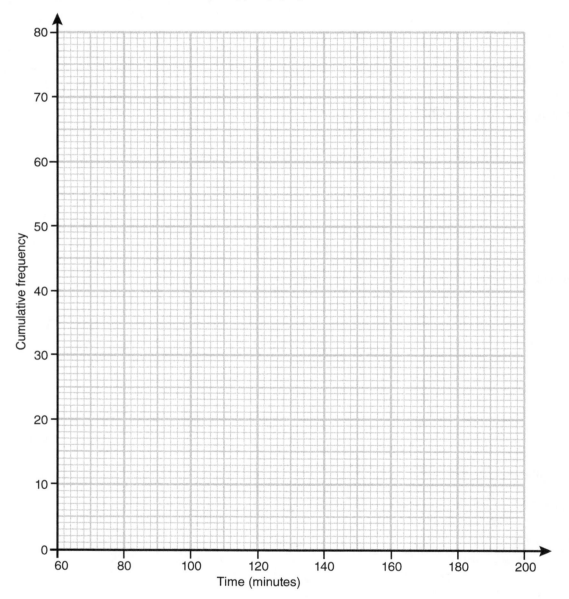

(b) Estimate the median film length for the month.   (1)

.... minutes

19 Nigel has a rectangular garden.

A surveyor estimates the area of his garden to be $42.5\,\text{m}^2$ to 1 decimal place.

Nigel measures the length of his garden as $9.32\,\text{m}$ to the nearest centimetre.

Find the maximum width of his garden to 3 significant figures. **(3)**

.... m

20 The nth term rule for a geometric sequence is $(1 + \sqrt{5})^n$

Write down the first three terms of the sequence in the form $a + \sqrt{b}$ **(3)**

....

21 Write down the coordinates for the turning point of the graph $y + 6x = x^2 + 11$ **(3)**

(.............., ...)

22 *ADC* is a straight line.

DC = 10.8 cm

BC = 12.3 cm

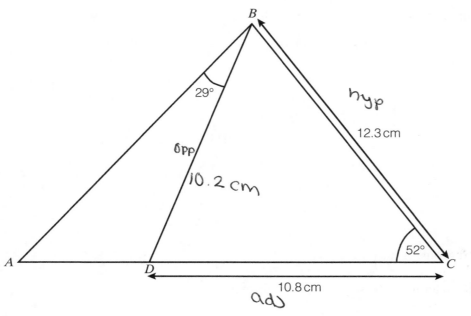

Find angle *BAD*.

Give your answer to 1 decimal place.   (5)

cosine
——————

$a^2 + b^2 - 2bc \cos A$

$12.3^2 + 10.8^2 - 2 \times 10.8 \times 12.3 \times \cos 52$

$= 104$

$\sqrt{}$

$= 10.2$

.... °

Name: ....

GCSE
Mathematics
Higher tier

H

Paper 1 (Non-Calculator)

Time: 1 hour 30 minutes

You must have: Ruler, protractor,
pair of compasses, pen, HB pencil, eraser.

Instructions

- Use **black** ink or black ball-point pen. Draw diagrams in pencil.
- Diagrams are **NOT** accurately drawn, unless otherwise indicated.
- Answer **all** questions.
- Answer the questions in the space provided.
- **Calculators may not be used**.
- You must **show all your working out**. Use a separate sheet of paper if needed.

Information

- The total mark for this paper is 80.
- The marks for **each** question are shown in brackets. Use this as a guide as to how much time to spend on each question.

Advice

- Read each question carefully before you start to answer it.
- Keep an eye on the time.
- Try to answer every question.
- Check your answers if you have time at the end.

1   (a) Write down 4.2×10^{-3} as an ordinary number.   (1)

....

    (b) Write down the calculation needed to decrease £350 by 12%   (1)

....

    (c) Find the area of a square with side length 1.2 m.   (1)

.... cm²

2   (a) Solve $\frac{2x}{3} = 5$ (1)

                                              $x =$ ....

    (b) Expand and simplify $(2x - 3)(x + 4)$ (2)

....

    (c) Factorise $a^2b - ab$ (2)

....

3   Work out 27×2.36 (3)

....

4 Solve $5(x - 4) = 3x - 15$ **(2)**

$x =$ ....

5 **(a)** Convert $\frac{3}{11}$ to a decimal number.   **(2)**

....

(b) Find $\frac{3}{5}$ of $3\frac{3}{4}$ **(3)**

....

6 Julie set up a video camera in her garden. Over 30 nights she recorded how many different times she captured some wild animals. Here are her results:

Animal	Frequency (number of nights seen)
Fox	8
Badger	2
Owl	3
Stoat	5
Hedgehog	11
Other rodent	12

(a) On any given night, find the probability that Julie will record a fox.   **(1)**

....

(b) On any given night, find the probability that she will record an owl and a stoat.   **(2)**

....

7 There are 350 trees in a forest. After strong winds there are only 280 left standing.

What percentage of trees has been destroyed? **(2)**

....%

8 The table shows the salary of five midwives and the number of years that they have worked.

Years	2	5	3	11	8
Salary	£22 500	£28 000	£24 000	£31 500	£30 000

(a) Draw a scatter graph to represent this information. **(2)**

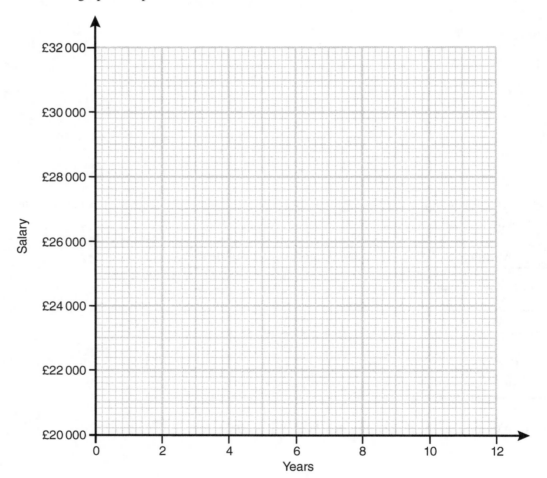

(b) Estimate the salary of a midwife who has been working for six years. **(1)**

£..

(c) Explain why the graph would not be suitable to estimate the salary of a midwife who has been working for 20 years. **(1)**

....

....

9 30 000 people have booked tickets for a music festival. Steph will be selling tents at the festival. Out of a sample of 600 people, 100 people indicated that they will require a tent when they get there.

Work out how many tents Steph should have in stock for the festival. Write down any assumptions which you make. **(3)**

.... tents

10 Here are two shapes, A and B.

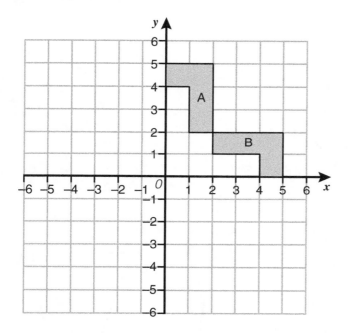

(a) Describe fully the transformation which maps Shape A onto Shape B. **(2)**

....

....

(b) Rotate Shape A 90° anticlockwise about the point (–1, 1). **(2)**

11   Jonathon is driving from Manchester (M) to Stoke-on-Trent (S). On the way, he stops off at Knutsford services (K). The total distance for the journey from Manchester to Stoke-on-Trent is 66 miles.

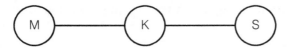

The journey from Manchester to Knutsford services takes 40 minutes and Jonathon travels at an average speed of 51 mph. The journey from Knutsford services to Stoke-on-Trent takes 30 minutes.

Find his average speed in the second part of the journey.   **(3)**

.... mph

12   Here are four triangles: *ABC*, *DEF*, *GHI* and *JKL*.

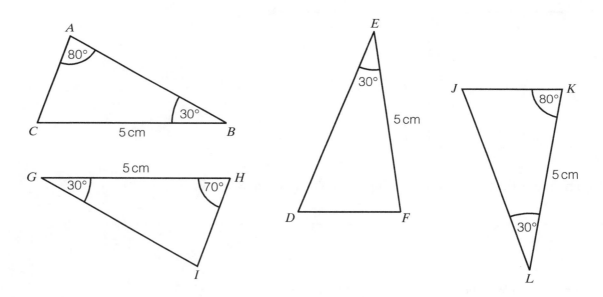

Which two triangles are congruent? Give reasons.   **(2)**

....

....

....

13 This quadrant has radius $2x$.

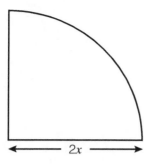

$\longleftarrow$ $2x$ $\longrightarrow$

Find the perimeter of the quadrant. Give your answer in terms of x and π. **(2)**

....

14 Rahab buys a car for £16 000. This included a 20% discount.

Rahab says, "The car would have cost £19 200 at full price."

Is Rahab correct? Show your working. **(2)**

....

15 $a = \begin{pmatrix} -2 \\ q \end{pmatrix}$ $\qquad$ $b = \begin{pmatrix} r \\ 8 \end{pmatrix}$ $\qquad$ $a + 2b = \begin{pmatrix} 4 \\ 21 \end{pmatrix}$

Write down the value of q and r. **(2)**

$q = $ ....

$r = $ ....

16 **(a)** Factorise $16x^2 - 169$ **(2)**

....

(b) Solve $x^2 - 9x - 36 = 0$ **(2)**

$x =$ .... and $x =$ ....

17 Kevin walks from Land's End to John O'Groats. He calculates that the distance is 880 miles to the nearest 5 miles.

Write down the error interval for the distance in miles, m. **(2)**

....

18 Find the equation of the line which is perpendicular to the line $y = 3x - 2$ and passes through the point (4, 0). **(3)**

....

19 Kash is listening to radio signals from space. He spots the following pattern:

3, 11, 23, 39, 59, 83 …

If the pattern continues like this, what will the 100th term in the sequence be? (4)

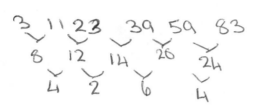

....

20 An Olympic size swimming pool is a cuboid with a volume of 2500 m³. It covers a floor area of 1250 m².

A mathematically similar pool is to be made with a volume of 2000 m³.

Find the floor area of the smaller pool. Give your answer to the nearest square metre. (4)

....m²

21 Write down all the integers, x, which satisfy $x^2 - 5x - 6 \leqslant 0$ (4)

....

22   The vertical height of this square-based pyramid is $\sqrt{a}$.

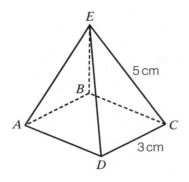

      Find the value of a.   (4)

                                           $a =$ ....

23   The probability of Event A happening is $\dfrac{7}{3x}$

      The probability of Event B happening is $\dfrac{6x}{x-1}$

      Find the probability of Event A and Event B happening. Write your answer in its simplest form.   (3)

      ....

24 50 people in a bike shop are asked what type of bike they own.

The Venn diagram shows the results of the survey.

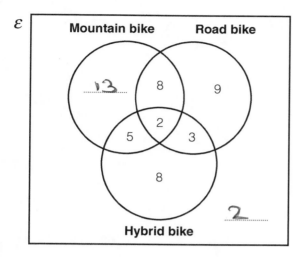

28 people own a mountain bike.

(a) Complete the Venn diagram. **(1)**

(b) What is the probability that someone who owns a road bike also owns a mountain bike? **(1)**

$$\frac{8}{50} = \frac{4}{25}$$

$$\frac{4}{25}$$

(c) What is the probability that someone who owns a hybrid bike also owns a mountain bike and a road bike? **(1)**

$$\frac{2}{50} = \frac{1}{25}$$

$$\frac{1}{25}$$

25 Show that $\left(\frac{\sqrt{3}+1}{4}\right)^{-1}$ can be written in the form $a\sqrt{b} - a$, where a and b are integers. **(4)**

TOTAL FOR PAPER IS 80 MARKS

Name: ....

GCSE

Mathematics

Higher tier

H

Paper 2 (Calculator)

Time: 1 hour 30 minutes

You must have: Ruler, protractor, pair of compasses, pen, HB pencil, eraser, calculator.

Instructions

- Use **black** ink or black ball-point pen. Draw diagrams in pencil.
- Diagrams are **NOT** accurately drawn, unless otherwise indicated.
- Answer **all** questions.
- Answer the questions in the space provided.
- **Calculators may be used**.
- If your calculator does not have a π button, take the value of π to be 3.142 unless the question instructs otherwise.
- You must **show all your working out**. Use a separate sheet of paper if needed.

Information

- The total mark for this paper is 80.
- The marks for **each** question are shown in brackets. Use this as a guide as to how much time to spend on each question.

Advice

- Read each question carefully before you start to answer it.
- Keep an eye on the time.
- Try to answer every question.
- Check your answers if you have time at the end.

1   (a) Given that $a = 3$ and $b = -4$, find the value of $\dfrac{a-b}{b^2}$ **(1)**

....

(b) Simplify $2a - (3b + a) - 2b$ **(1)**

....

2   Last year, Instatwitt had 1 372 658 users. This year it has 1 587 392 users.

What percentage increase is this? Give your answer to 1 decimal place.   **(2)**

....%

3   Jessica and Peter share shoelace sweets in the ratio of 11 : 15

Peter gets two more sweets than Jessica. A shoelace sweet can be split in half.

How many sweets does Peter get?   **(3)**

.... sweets

4 162 students in Year 10 are having a reward day.

- 66.$\dot{6}$% are going to a theme park.

- $\frac{8}{27}$ are going ice-skating.

- The rest are staying in school.

How many students are staying in school? **(4)**

.... students

5 **(a)** Write the first five terms of the following term-to-term sequence.

 'Start with the first prime number, then add five each time.' **(1)**

....

 (b) Find the nth term rule for the sequence. **(2)**

....

 (c) Find the 27th term in the sequence. **(1)**

....

6 A sector is drawn in one corner of a regular decagon with side length 5 cm.

The radius of the sector is equal to one side of the decagon.

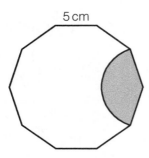

5 cm

Find the area of the shaded sector. Leave your answer in terms of π. **(4)**

.... cm²

7 A wedding venue uses eight chefs to prepare a meal for 140 guests.

(a) How many chefs would be needed to prepare a meal for 175 guests? **(2)**

.... chefs

(b) Write down one assumption which you have made. **(1)**

....

....

8   An ice-cube tray holds 16 ice cubes with side length 2 cm.

Shiv tips all 16 ice cubes into a cylindrical jug with diameter 12 cm.

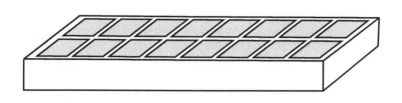 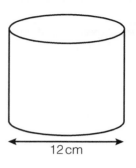

12 cm

What will be the height of the water in the jug once the ice has melted? Give your answer to
3 significant figures. **(4)**

.... cm

9   The coordinates of the apex of triangle A are (7, 1).

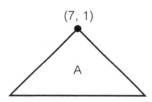

(7, 1)

A

Triangle A is translated with the vector $\begin{pmatrix} 2 \\ -5 \end{pmatrix}$ to map it onto triangle B.

(a) Write down the coordinates of the apex of triangle B. **(2)**

(................, ...)

(b) A straight line passes through the apex of the two triangles.

Find the equation of the line. **(3)**

10 A film cost £1.25 × 10⁷ to make.

At the box office the film made £6.32 × 10⁸

(a) How much profit did the film make? Write your answer in standard form. **(2)**

£ ....

The lead actress was paid $2.1 \times 10^{-1}\%$ of the profits.

(b) How much was the lead actress paid? Write your answer as an ordinary number. **(2)**

£ ....

11 **(a)** Sketch the graph of $y = x^2 + 3x + 2$ **(2)**

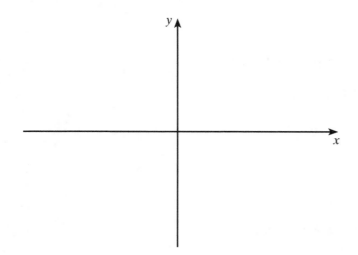

(b) Hence, or otherwise, write down the coordinates of the turning point of $y = x^2 + 3x + 2$ **(1)**

(.............. , ...)

12 A man is standing at the top of some vertical cliffs looking out to sea.

His measuring instrument can measure the angle of depression and the distance from himself to a boat.

The angle of depression is 62°.

The distance is 658 m.

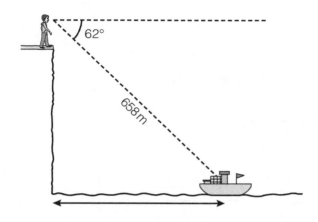

Find the horizontal distance from the boat to the cliffs. Give your answer to 2 decimal places. (3)

.... m

13 (a) Evaluate $\dfrac{6^7 \times 6^{-2}}{6^6}$ (2)

....

(b) Find the value of x when $8^x = 16$ (2)

$x =$ ....

14 Prove that $0.1\dot{3}\dot{6}$ can be written as $\frac{3}{22}$ (3)

15 Four people were given several puzzles to solve.

The box plots summarise the time taken to complete the individual puzzles.

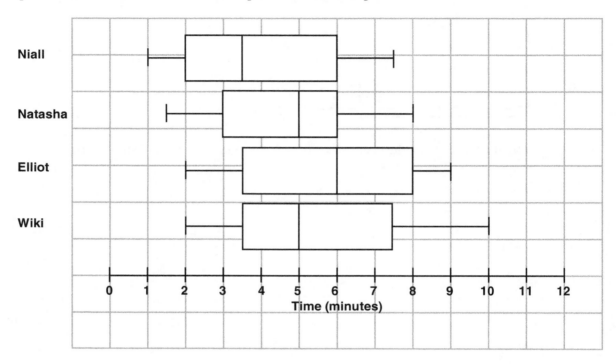

(a) Which person was the least consistent? Give a reason for your answer. (1)

....

....

....

(b) Write down one similarity between two of the people.

Use figures to back up your answer. (2)

....

....

....

....

16 Solve the equation $x = \dfrac{2}{5x - 4}$

Give your answer to 2 decimal places. **(5)**

$x =$ .... and $x =$ ....

17 A marine biologist is measuring the speed of a great white shark while it is hunting.

The graph shows its speed over 8 seconds.

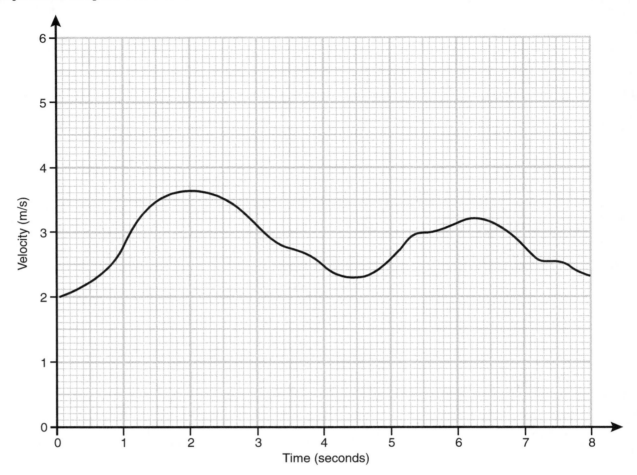

(a) Calculate the acceleration of the shark at exactly 4 seconds. **(3)**

.... m/s^2

(b) How far does the shark travel between 6 and 8 seconds? **(2)**

.... m

18 In a competition, drummers attempted to play the most beats per second.

The histogram and frequency table illustrate the results.

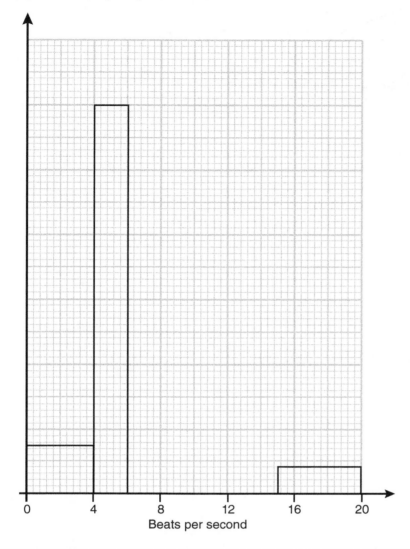

Beats per second, b	$0 < b \leqslant 4$	$4 < b \leqslant 6$	$6 < b \leqslant 12$	$12 < b \leqslant 15$	$15 < b \leqslant 20$
Frequency			10	7	2

(a) Complete the histogram and frequency table. (2)

(b) Half of the drummers qualified.

   Estimate how many beats per minute were needed to qualify. (2)

.... beats per minute

19 The area of the triangle is 10.15 cm².

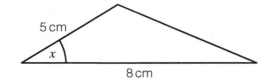

Find the angle marked x. Give your answer to 3 significant figures.   (3)

$x =$ ....°

20 Find the non-integer solutions to the simultaneous equations

$3x^2 + y^2 = 139$

$2x + y = 18$ (5)

$x =$ ....

$y =$ ....

21 Set A and Set B are inside the universal set ε.

ε = {$x: 0 < x \leq 15$}

Set A = {$x: 0 < x \leq 15$ and x is even}

Set B = {$x: 0 < x \leq 15$ and x is a multiple of 3}

Complete the Venn diagram to show the universal set ε. (3)

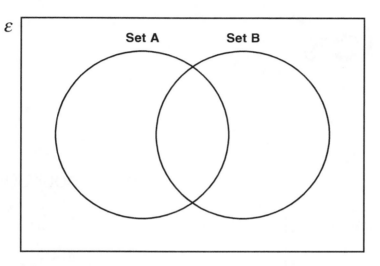

22 There are 12 boys and 13 girls in a class.

Three students are to be chosen at random to take part in an open evening.

Find the probability that at least one boy will be chosen. (4)

TOTAL FOR PAPER IS 80 MARKS

Name: ....

GCSE
Mathematics
Higher tier

H

Paper 3 (Calculator)

Time: 1 hour 30 minutes

You must have: Ruler, protractor, pair of compasses, pen, HB pencil, eraser, calculator.

Instructions

- Use **black** ink or black ball-point pen. Draw diagrams in pencil.
- Diagrams are **NOT** accurately drawn, unless otherwise indicated.
- Answer **all** questions.
- Answer the questions in the space provided.
- **Calculators may be used**.
- If your calculator does not have a π button, take the value of π to be 3.142 unless the question instructs otherwise.
- You must **show all your working out**. Use a separate sheet of paper if needed.

Information

- The total mark for this paper is 80.
- The marks for **each** question are shown in brackets. Use this as a guide as to how much time to spend on each question.

Advice

- Read each question carefully before you start to answer it.
- Keep an eye on the time.
- Try to answer every question.
- Check your answers if you have time at the end.

1   Write down whether each statement is true or false.

Give a reason for your answer.

(a) The value of x^3 is **always** positive.   **(1)**

....

....

....

(b) The value of x^2 is **always** positive.   **(1)**

....

....

....

(c) The value of x^2 is **never** equal to the value of $2x$.   **(1)**

....

....

....

2   **(a)** Solve the inequality $-6 \leqslant 2x - 3 < 3$ **(2)**

....

(b) Write down all of the integers which satisfy $-6 \leqslant 2x - 3 < 3$ **(1)**

....

3   Clive wants to find out how often students visit the library. He questions a selection of students at random.

(a) Write down two mathematical words which describe Clive's data.   (2)

....

....

(b) Describe what it means to select students at random.   (1)

....

....

4   Here are four circles, with the centre point marked.

A
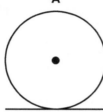

B

C
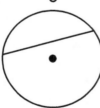

D
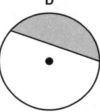

Write down the letter of the diagram which shows:

(a) A sector   ....   (1)

(b) A tangent   ....   (1)

5 Rachel is the exams officer at a school. She finds that 38 out of 203 pupils do not bring a calculator to the maths exam.

(a) Out of 48 752 students taking the maths exam in England, estimate how many will not bring a calculator to the exam. **(2)**

.... students

(b) Have you made an over-estimate or an under-estimate?

State any assumptions you have made. **(2)**

....

....

....

6 Violet wants to invest £2500 for three years. She looks at two different options:

Premium bonds
For every £1000 you invest, you are likely to receive a cheque for £15 per year. (This is not compound interest).

Local bank (compound interest)
• 1% interest for the first year.
• 1.5% interest for the second year.
• 2% interest for the third year.

Which option is likely to give the most money if Violet invests £2500 for three years? **(5)**

....

7 Shape $ABCD$ is a quadrilateral such that:

$AB = BC = BD$

$BAC = 3x°$

$BCD = 4x°$

$CBD = 32°$

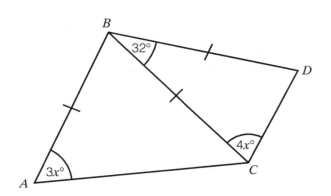

Find the value of the missing angle ABC. **(4)**

....°

8 On a film set, the canteen offered four different meals. The probabilities that the different meals were chosen by the crew members are shown in the table.

Meal	Pie and chips	Chicken stir-fry	Salmon risotto	Vegetarian option
Probability	$18x$	$8x$	$11x$	$3x$

(a) What percentage of the crew chose salmon risotto? **(3)**

....%

There are 80 crew members in total.

(b) How many chose the vegetarian option? **(2)**

....

9   Matt took part in a 10 km run. He burns 133 calories for every mile he runs.

The run took him 1 hour and 15 minutes to complete. His usual average speed on level tarmac is 9 miles per hour (mph).

(a) How many calories did Matt burn on the run?   **(4)**

.... calories

(b) Select which of the following, A, B, C or D, best describes the 10 km run. Give reasons for your answer.

    A: Streets and pavements around town, with no hills

    B: A cross-country run with muddy, rocky paths and steep inclines

    C: Several laps around a running track

    D: A run along a sandy beach   **(3)**

....

....

....

....

....

....

10 A chocolate in the shape of a sphere has a mint crème filling.

The radius of the sphere is 5 mm.

The ratio of chocolate to mint crème filling is 3 : 5

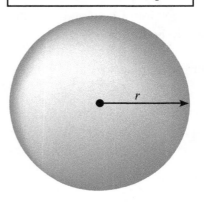

Volume of a sphere $= \frac{4}{3}\pi r^3$

Find the volume of mint crème filling. Give your answer to 1 decimal place. **(4)**

....mm^3

11 Shape $ABCD$ is a kite.

M is the midpoint of DB.

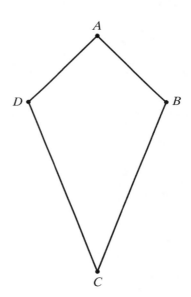

Prove that triangle AMD is congruent to triangle AMB. **(3)**

12 A function is represented by the following function machine:

Input $\longrightarrow$ | $\times 6$ | $\longrightarrow$ | $- 6$ | $\longrightarrow$ Output

When the input is a, the output is b.

Use this information to solve the equation $4a - b = 3$ **(4)**

$a = \text{...}$

$b = \text{...}$

13 Joel and Isaac play the game Rock–Paper–Scissors. They each shake a hand simultaneously and create the shape of a rock, paper or scissors with it.

- Rock beats scissors
- Paper beats rock
- Scissors beat paper

They play the best out of three handshakes.

Find the probability that Joel wins the first two handshakes. **(3)**

14 $x^2 + bx + c$ can be written in the form $(x + D)^2 + E$

Find D and E in terms of b and c. **(3)**

$D =$ ....

$E =$ ....

15 The cumulative frequency graph shows the heights of rides at a travelling fun fair.

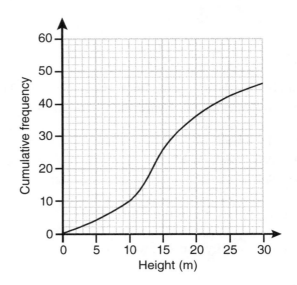

(a) Estimate the percentage of rides below 15 m in height. **(2)**

....%

(b) A certain venue will not allow rides above 20 m in height.

Estimate how many rides the fun fair will not be able to set up. **(2)**

.... rides

16 *P*, *Q* and *R* are points on the circumference of a circle.

O is the centre of the circle.

Find angle *PQR* in terms of *x*. Give a reason for your answer. **(3)**

....°

....

....

....

17 The functions f(x) and g(x) are given by the following:

f(x) = $x^2 - 2$

g(x) = $5 - 3x$

(a) Write the function f^{-1}(x) (2)

f^{-1}(x) = ...

(b) Find the value of fg(5) (2)

....

18 The length of the hypotenuse of a right-angled isosceles triangle is 40 cm.

The length of another side can be written as $a\sqrt{b}$ cm.

Find the values of a and b. (4)

a = ...

b = ...

19 The length of runway needed for a jet airliner to land is directly proportional to the square of its speed at touchdown.

A jet airliner which touches down at 240 kph needs 2000 m of runway.

Find the speed, at touchdown, of a jet airliner which uses 2400 m of runway to land.
Give your answer to 3 significant figures. **(4)**

.... kph

20 The function $y = f(x)$ is shown on the diagram.

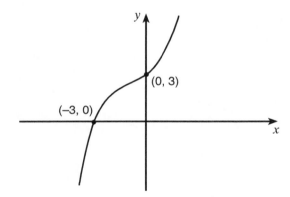

(a) On the graph above, make a sketch of the function $y = f(x - 3)$ **(1)**

(b) Give the coordinates of two points on the graph of $y = f(x - 3)$ **(2)**

(.............., ...) and (.............., ...)

21 A frustum is made by removing a small cone from the top of a larger cone.

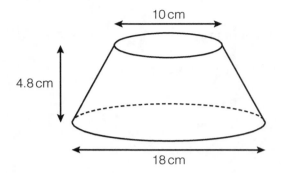

Find the height of the larger cone which was used to make this frustum. **(5)**

.... cm

TOTAL FOR PAPER IS 80 MARKS

──────────────────── **END OF PRACTICE EXAM 2** ────────────────────

You are encouraged to show your working out, as you may be awarded marks for method even if your final answer is wrong. Full marks can be awarded where a correct answer is given without working being shown, but if a question asks for working out, you must show it to gain full marks. If you use a correct method that is not shown in the mark scheme below, you would still gain full credit for it.

PRACTICE EXAM 1

Paper 1 (pages 3–14)

1. (a) $\frac{21}{35} + \frac{10}{35}$ [1] $= \frac{31}{35}$ [1]

> Use the lowest common multiple of 5 and 7 (= 35) as the denominator.

 (b) $\frac{3}{4} \times \frac{3}{2}$ [1] $= \frac{9}{8}$ [1] $= 1\frac{1}{8}$ [1]

> Find the reciprocal of the second fraction and multiply.

2. $x^{3 \times 4} = x^{12}$

> Multiply the powers.

3. $200 \div 5$ [1] = £40 per share [1]

> Mathilda gets five more shares than Clarisse.

 Charlotte = £160 (4 × £40), Clarisse = £240 (6 × £40), Mathilda = £440 (11 × £40) [1]

4. $BCD = 68°$ (alternate angles are equal) [1]
 $CBD = 56°$ (isosceles triangle has equal base angles) [1]
 $ABD = 124°$ (angles on a straight line sum to 180°), $DAB = 34°$ (angles in a triangle sum to 180°) [1]
 $x = 360 - 68 - 34 = 258°$ (angles around a point) [1]

5. (a) Either $\frac{2}{7}$ (Tim's results), $\frac{11}{31}$ (Amanda's results)
 or $\frac{13}{38}$ (combined) [1 mark for each correct up to a maximum of 2]

 (b) Either Amanda's or combined, depending on answer to part (a).
 Reason: More days being recorded will give a more accurate estimate.

6. (a) $170 < h \leqslant 175$

 (b) Median $= \frac{(117 + 1)}{2} = $ 59th person [1]
 $175 < h \leqslant 180$ [1]

> Add up the frequencies until you get to 59.

7. (a) $2x - 4 \leqslant 7$ [1 mark for correct first step]
 $2x \leqslant 11$
 $x \leqslant 5.5$ [1]

> Solve the inequality like an ordinary equation.

 (b)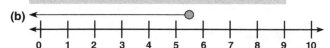

 [1 mark for correct line segment; 1 mark for shaded circle. (2 marks for the correct diagram based on incorrect part (a))]

8. $610\,000 + 42\,000 = 652\,000$ [1]
 6.52×10^5 [1]

9. $8x^2 - 4x + 12x - 6$ [1]
 $8x^2 + 8x - 6$ [1]

10. (a) Gradient = 3 or y-intercept = (0, 2) [1]
 $y = 3x + 2$ [1]

 (b) $y = 3x + c$

 > Substitute the point (3, 2) into the equation to find c.

 $2 = 3 \times 3 + c$ [1]
 $c = -7$
 $y = 3x - 7$ [1]

11. £180\,000 = 120% [1]
 £1500 = 1%
 £150\,000 = 100% [1]

12. 15 men = 18 days' work
 1 man = 270 days' work [1]
 12 men = 22.5 days [1]

 > Multiply by 15 and then divide by 12.

13. $10 \div 4 = 2.5$ [1]
 $AB = 7.5 \div 2.5 = 3\,cm$ [1]
 $AC = 5\,cm$ [1]
 $AE = 5 \times 2.5 = 12.5\,cm$ [1]
 $CE = 12.5 - 5 = 7.5\,cm$ [1]

 > AC is 5 cm since ABC is a (3, 4, 5) triangle, using Pythagoras.

14. (a)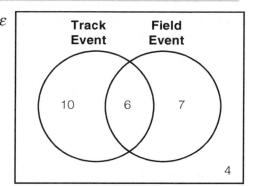

 [2 marks if fully correct; 1 mark for at least two correct values]

 (b) $\frac{6}{27}$ [2] [1 mark for either 6 or 27 identified]

15. $(p + 1) \times q = 5 + 7p$ [1]
 $pq + q = 5 + 7p$
 $pq - 7p = 5 - q$
 $p(q - 7) = 5 - q$ [1]
 $p = \frac{5 - q}{q - 7}$ or $p = \frac{q - 5}{7 - q}$ [1]

16. He has a lower median (45 seconds compared to 47 seconds), meaning on average he is faster. [1]
 He has a smaller range (10 seconds compared to 12 seconds), meaning he is more consistent.
 He has a smaller interquartile range (5 seconds compared to 6 seconds), meaning he is more consistent. [1 mark for a statement about range or interquartile range]

17. $x = 0.3\dot{2}\dot{7}$
 $10x = 3.\dot{2}\dot{7}$
 $1000x = 327.\dot{2}\dot{7}$ [1 mark for any of these three statements]

Answers

$990x = 324$ **[1]**

$x = \frac{324}{990}$

$x = \frac{18}{55}$ **[1]**

> $1000x - 10x$ will eliminate the recurring decimals.

18. $\left(\frac{81}{16}\right)^{\frac{3}{4}}$ **[1]**

$\left(\frac{3}{2}\right)^3$ **[1]**

$\frac{27}{8} = 3\frac{3}{8}$ **[1]**

> Find the fourth root of 81 and 16 and then cube 3 and 2.

19. $\frac{1}{2} \times a \times \sqrt{3} \times \sin 60° = 1.5\,\text{cm}^2$ **[1]**

$\frac{1}{2} \times a \times \sqrt{3} \times \frac{\sqrt{3}}{2} = 1.5\,\text{cm}^2$ **[1]**

$\frac{3}{4}\,a = 1.5\,\text{cm}^2$ **[1]**

$a = 2\,\text{cm}$ **[1]**

20. (a)

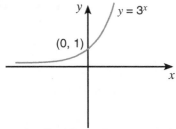

[1 mark for a curve tending to 0 in the negative axis; 1 mark for intercept marked at (0, 1)]

(b) $y = 2\cos(x)$ **[2]**

[1 mark for $y = \cos(x)$]

21. (a) $\left(\frac{1}{2} \times 40 \times 20\right) + (40 \times 20) + \left(\frac{1}{2} \times 50 \times 20\right)$
$+ (20 \times 30) + \left(\frac{1}{2} \times 60 \times 30\right)$ **[1]**

$400 + 800 + 500 + 600 + 900 = 3200\,\text{m}$ **[1]**

$3.2\,\text{km}$ **[1]**

> Find the area under the graph.

(b) $0.5\,\text{m/s}^2$, $0\,\text{m/s}^2$, $0.5\,\text{m/s}^2$, $0\,\text{m/s}^2$ and $-0.5\,\text{m/s}^2$

[2 marks for any two correct accelerations]

22. $\frac{x+2}{x} \times \left(\frac{x-1}{x-1}\right) - \frac{x}{x-1} \times \left(\frac{x}{x}\right)$ **[1]**

$\frac{(x+2)(x-1) - x^2}{x(x-1)}$ **[1]**

$\frac{x^2 + 2x - x - 2 - x^2}{x(x-1)} = \frac{x-2}{x(x-1)}$ **[1]**

23.

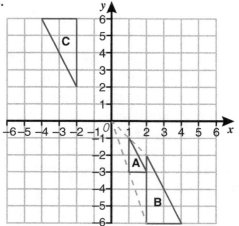

(a) Triangle B with vertices $(2, -2)$, $(2, -6)$ and $(4, -6)$ **[1]**

Triangle C with vertices $(-4, 6)$, $(-2, 6)$ and $(-2, 2)$ **[1]**

(b) Enlargement with scale factor -2 **[1]** about $(0, 0)$ **[1]**.

24. $\text{fg}(x) = (3x + 5)^2 + 2$ **[1]**

$\text{fg}(x) = (9x^2 + 15x + 15x + 25) + 2$ **[1]**

$\text{fg}(x) = 9x^2 + 30x + 27$ **[1]**

> Substitute $(3x + 5)$ into $x^2 + 2$

25. $3y = 13 - 2x$

$2x + 3y = 13$ **[1]**

$(2, 3)$ **[1]**

> The equation of the tangent line at the point (h, k) is $hx + ky = r^2$

Paper 2 (pages 15–27)

1. (a) $4x(3x - 1)$ **(b)** $12x^3y^2$ **(c)** $3 \times (-2)^2 - (-2) = 14$

2. (a) $\frac{4^3}{\sqrt{100} - 6}$ **[1]** $= \frac{64}{4} = 16$ **[1]**

> Round all the figures to 1 significant figure.

(b) $\frac{59.319}{3.678699101} = 16.12499375$

> Do not round at any point.

(c) 16.1

3. (a) £450 × 1.285 **[1]** = €578.25 **[1]**

(b) France: 36 ÷ 1.285 = £28.02 **[1]**

£28.02 − £27 = £1.02 **[1]**

4. (a) $\frac{1}{2}(5^2 + 5) = 15$

$\frac{1}{2}(6^2 + 6) = 21$

15 **[1]** and 21 **[1]**

(b) 1, 3, 6, 10, 15, 21, ... **[1 mark for at least three of 1, 3, 6 and 10 found]**

Triangular numbers **[1]**

> Substitute $n = 1, 2, 3, 4$, etc. into the nth term rule to get the sequence.

5. Beans: 14, 28, 42, **56**, 70, 84

Soup: 8, 16, 24, 32, 40, 48, **56**, 64

[1 mark for listing multiples of 14 and 8; 1 mark for finding a common multiple of 8 and 14, e.g. 56, 112, etc.]

4 boxes of beans and 7 boxes of soup (or any multiples of 4 and 7) **[1]**

6. 500 g + 1000 g + 1500 g = 3000 g

3000 g ÷ 2170 cm³ **[1]** = 1.38 g/cm³ **[1]**

> Convert all amounts into grams and cm³.

7. Dionne: $\frac{14}{27} = 0.51851... = 51.9\%$ boys **[1]**

Claire: $\frac{5}{9} = 0.555555... = 55.6\%$ boys **[1]**

Emily: $100\% - 46\% = 54\%$ boys

Claire has the biggest proportion of boys. **[1]**

> Use a calculator to convert the fractions into decimals.

8. (a) £152 000 × (1.02)¹ **[1]** × (1.025)² **[1]** = £162 888.90 **[1]**

(b) 4 years later: £162 888.90 × (1.025)⁴

$= £179\,798.87 < £180\,000$

5 years later: £162 888.90 × (1.025)⁵

$= £184\,293.84 > £180\,000$

2018 + 5 years = 2023

> Use trial and improvement for different numbers of years.

9. (a) 1

(b) $\frac{1}{2^5}$ **[1]** $= \frac{1}{32}$ **[1]**

10. Equation 1: $15x + 10y = 25$

Equation 2: $15x - 21y = 63.75$

Equation 1 – Equation 2: $31y = -38.75$ **[1]**

$y = -1.25$

$3x + 2(-1.25) = 5$ **[1]**

$3x = 7.5$

$x = 2.5$, $y = -1.25$ **[1]**

> Substitute the y-value into one of the original equations.

11. Volume of cone $= \frac{1}{3} \times \pi \times 3^2 \times 9 = 27\pi$ **[1]**

Volume of sphere = volume of cone: $\frac{4}{3}\pi r^3 = 27\pi$ **[1]**

$r^3 = 20.25$ **[1]**

$r = \sqrt[3]{20.25} = 2.73\,\text{cm}$ **[1]**

12. $\sin 63° = \frac{18}{RS}$ **[1]**

$RS = \frac{18}{\sin 63°}$ **[1]**

$RS = 20.2\,\text{cm}$ **[1]**

13. (a)

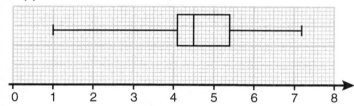

```
0   1   2   3   4   5   6   7   8
```

[3 marks if fully correct; 2 marks for only one error;
1 mark for box correct or whiskers correct]

> Draw the upper quartile, median and lower quartile
> onto the cumulative frequency graph at 45, 30 and 15
> respectively.

(b) Any one of the following: The range is 6.2m; The
median is 4.5m; The interquartile range is $5.4 - 4.1 = 1.3\,\text{m}$

14. $4 \times 12 \times 7 + 1 \times 10 \times 7$ **[1]** $= 406$ **[1]**

> Four sizes have all colours and designs available; one
> size has only 10 designs available.

15. (a) $PQR = 180° - 116° = 64°$ **[1]**

Reason: Opposite angles in a cyclic quadrilateral add
up to 180°. **[1]**

(b) $QPR = QRU = 58°$ **[1]**

Reason: The angle in the alternate segment is equal. **[1]**

> Notice that triangle QPR is isosceles.

16. $x \propto \frac{1}{\sqrt{y}}$

$x = \frac{k}{\sqrt{y}}$ **[1]**

$0.5 = \frac{k}{\sqrt{25}}$

$k = 2.5$ **[1]**

$x = \frac{2.5}{\sqrt{y}}$

$25 = \frac{2.5}{\sqrt{y}}$

$\sqrt{y} = \frac{2.5}{25}$

$\sqrt{y} = 0.1$

$y = 0.1^2 = 0.01$ **[1]**

17.

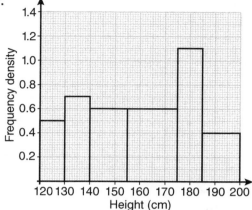

Height (cm)

> Frequency density = frequency ÷ class width
> ($5 \div 10 = 0.5$, $7 \div 10 = 0.7$, $9 \div 15 = 0.6$, $12 \div 20 = 0.6$,
> $11 \div 10 = 1.1$, $6 \div 15 = 0.4$)

**[1 mark for at least one frequency density found;
2 marks for at least three correct bars; 3 marks for a
complete and fully labelled graph]**

18. (a) $x^3 = 5x - 7$ **[1 mark for this correct step seen]**

which leads to the answer $x = \sqrt[3]{5x - 7}$

(b) $x_1 = \sqrt[3]{5(-2) - 7} = \sqrt[3]{-17} = -2.571281591$ **[1]**

$x_2 = \sqrt[3]{5(-2.571281591) - 7} = \sqrt[3]{-19.85640795}$

$= -2.707905861$ **[1]**

(c) $x_3 = -2.738609828$

$x_4 = -2.745416017$

$x_5 = -2.746920192$ **[1]**

$x_6 = -2.747252394$

$x = -2.75$ **[1]**

> Continue with iteration until the answer remains the
> same to 2 decimal places.

19. (a) $2n + 1$ is an odd number

$(2n + 1) + (2n + 3) + (2n + 5)$ **[1]**

$= 6n + 9$

$6n + 9 = 3(2n + 3)$ and therefore divisible by 3. **[1]**

(b) $(2n) \times (2n + 2) \times (2n + 4)$ **[1]**

$= (2n) \times (4n^2 + 12n + 8)$

$= (8n^3 + 24n^2 + 16n)$

$= 8(n^3 + 3n^2 + 2n)$ and therefore divisible by 8. **[1]**

20. $0.8 \times 0.9 = 0.72$ **[1]**

$0.2 \times 0.6 = 0.12$ **[1]**

$0.72 + 0.12 = 0.84$ **[1]**

0.84×500 **[1]** $= 420$ seeds **[1]**

> Draw a tree diagram to show the probabilities.

21. $\overrightarrow{DB} = 3\mathbf{a} + 5\mathbf{b}$ **[1]**

$\overrightarrow{MN} = \overrightarrow{MA} + \overrightarrow{AN}$

$\overrightarrow{MN} = 2\mathbf{a} + \overrightarrow{AN}$

$\overrightarrow{AN} = \frac{2(5\mathbf{b})}{3}$ since $\overrightarrow{MN}$ and $\overrightarrow{DB}$ are parallel.

$\overrightarrow{NB} = \frac{1(5\mathbf{b})}{3}$ **[1]**

$\overrightarrow{NC} = \overrightarrow{NB} + \overrightarrow{BC}$ **[1]**

$\overrightarrow{NC} = \frac{1}{3}(5\mathbf{b}) + (-3\mathbf{a}) = \frac{5\mathbf{b}}{3} - 3\mathbf{a}$ **[1]**

22. Volume $= (2x + 3) \times (x - 1) \times (3x + 2)$ **[1]**

$= (2x^2 - 2x + 3x - 3)(3x + 2)$

$= (2x^2 + x - 3)(3x + 2)$ **[1]**

$= (6x^3 + 4x^2 + 3x^2 + 2x - 9x - 6)$

$= 6x^3 + 7x^2 - 7x - 6$ **[1]**

> Expand one pair of brackets first.

23.(a)

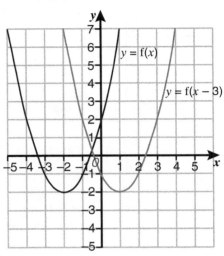

(b) $y = -f(x) + 2$ **[2]**   **[1 mark for either $-f(x)$ or $+ 2$]**

> The graph has been reflected in the x-axis and then translated up 2 units.

Paper 3 (pages 28–40)

1. Identity

2. (a) E   **(b)** C   **(c)** F

3. $0.035 \times 5450 = £190.75$ **[1]**

$£190.75 \times 4 = £763$ **[1]**

4. (a) $1260 = 2 \times 2 \times 3 \times 3 \times 5 \times 7$ **[2]** $= 2^2 \times 3^2 \times 5 \times 7$ **[1]**

[1 mark for first two correct steps using a prime factor tree]

> Use prime factor trees.

(b) $1050 = 2 \times 3 \times 5 \times 5 \times 7$

$1260 = 2 \times 2 \times 3 \times 3 \times 5 \times 7$

HCF $= 2 \times 3 \times 5 \times 7$ **[1]** $= 210$ **[1]**

> HCF is the product of the identical prime factors from each list.

5. (a) Any suitable answer, e.g.:

$5^2 = 25$, $25^3 = 15\,625$ **[1]**

$5^5 = 3125 \neq 15\,625$ **[1]**

Or Use algebra: $(x^2)^3 = x^6 \neq x^5$ **[1]**

Answer: No, with correct working seen **[1]**

(b) $\sqrt[3]{1771561} = 121$

$\sqrt{121} = 11$

Asif was thinking of 11.

> Work backwards; use a calculator.

6. C : D : J

$4 \times \frac{1}{3}J : \frac{1}{3}J : J$ **[1]**

$4 : 1 : 3$ **[1]**

> If Julien is one unit, Del is one-third and Carolyn is four lots of one-third.

7. (a) Circumference $= 4\pi x$ **[1]**

Perimeter $= 4\pi x + 3x + 4 + 3x + 4$ **[1]** $= 4\pi x + 6x + 8$

(b) $4\pi x + 6x + 8 = 652$ **[1]**

$4\pi x + 6x = 644$

$x(4\pi + 6) = 644$

$x = 644 \div (4\pi + 6) = 34.69$ **[1]**

8.

Time	10 s	20 s	30 s	40 s	**45 s**	50 s
Nat's distance	20 m	60 m	100 m	140 m	**160 m**	180 m
Tim's distance	0 m	0 m	40 m	120 m	**160 m**	200 m

[3 marks for full working leading to 160 m or 45 seconds: 2 marks for at least two areas calculated for each person; 1 mark for at least one area calculated]

The race was 160 m long. **[1]**

> Work out the area under each graph to find the distance.

9. (a) $360° - 45°$ **[1]** $= 315°$ **[1, allowing ± 2°]**

(b)

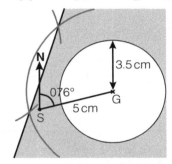

G marked at a bearing of 076° **[1]** where SG = 5 cm **[1]**

(c) Perpendicular bisector of RG drawn.

A circle, radius 3.5 cm, at G. **[1 for one correct construction]**

Correct region shaded **[1]**

10. Jill's mean: $(50 \times 3 + 150 \times 8 + 250 \times 6 + 350 \times 7)$

[1] $\div 24 = £220.83$ **[1]**

David's mean: $(50 \times 2 + 150 \times 4 + 250 \times 8 + 350 \times 6)$

[1] $\div 20 = £240$ **[1]**

David earned the most per painting. **[1]**

> Multiply the midpoints of each interval by the frequencies and divide by the total frequency.

11. (a)

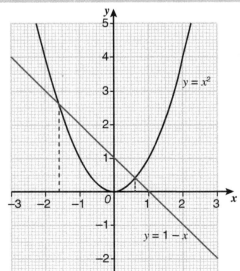

[2 marks for fully correct graph; 1 mark for correct y-intersect point (0, 1)]

(b) $x = 0.6$ **[1]** and $x = -1.6$ **[1]**

Read off the values for x where the two graphs intersect.

12. (a) First branch: 0.25 **[1]**

Second branch: 0.35, 0.65, 0.35 **[1]**

(b) P(Late, Late) = 0.25×0.35 **[1]** = 0.0875 **[1]**

13. (a) $20\,000 \times (0.85)^5$ **[1]** = 8874.106... tonnes **[1]**

(b) $20\,000 \times (p)^5 = 10\,000$ **[1]**

$p^5 = 0.5$

$p = \sqrt[5]{0.5} = 0.87055... = 87\%$ **[1]**

$100\% - 87\% = 13\%$ per year **[1]**

14.

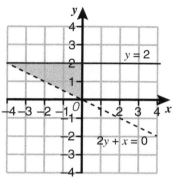

$y = 2$ drawn **[1]**

$2y + x = 0$ drawn **[1]**

Correct region shaded **[1]**

Rearrange the equation $2y + x = 0$ to make $y = -\frac{1}{2}x$

15. $BC^2 = 12^2 - 10.5^2$ **[1]**

$BC = \sqrt{33.75} = 5.809475019 \text{ cm}$ **[1]**

Area of triangle $ABC = \frac{1}{2} \times 5.809475019 \times 10.5$

$= 30.49974385 \text{ cm}^2$ **[1]**

Area of circle $= \pi \times 6^2 = 113.0973355 \text{ cm}^2$ **[1]**

$113.0973355 \text{ cm}^2 - 30.49974385 \text{ cm}^2 = 82.6 \text{ cm}^2$ **[1]**

Triangle ABC is a right-angled triangle since angles in a semi-circle are 90°.

16. (a)

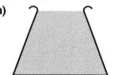

(b) $\frac{32}{2}$ **[1]** = 16 cm/s **[1]** **(acceptable range: 14–18 cm/s)**

Calculate the gradient of the tangent to the curve at 3 s.

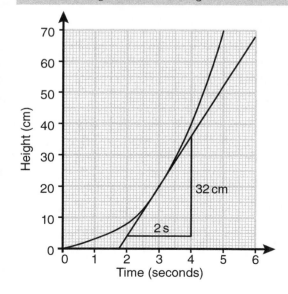

17. $2x^2 + 8x - 3 = 0$

$x = \frac{-8 \pm \sqrt{8^2 - 4 \times 2 \times -3}}{2 \times 2}$ **[1]**

$x = \frac{-8 \pm \sqrt{88}}{4}$ **[1]**

$x = 0.345$ and $x = -4.345$ **[1]**

Use the quadratic formula $x = \frac{-b \pm \sqrt{b^2 - 4ac}}{2a}$, when $ax^2 + bx + c = 0$

18. (a) Cumulative frequencies calculated: 4, 21, 39, 52, 60, 64

[1 mark, implied by fully correct graph]

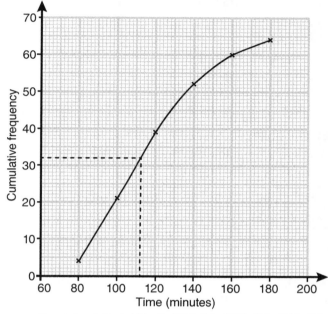

6 points plotted: (80, 4), (100, 21), (120, 39), (140, 52), (160, 60), (180, 64) and joined with a smooth curve

[2 marks if graph fully correct; 1 mark for at least five points plotted correctly]

(b) Median = 112 minutes **(accept 111 to 113)**

Draw a line at exactly 32 on the cumulative frequency graph.

19. Area upper bound = 42.55 m² and length lower bound = 9.315 m **[1 mark for one correct bound]**

Maximum width = $\frac{42.55}{9.315}$ **[1]** = 4.57 m **[1]**

20. 1st term: $(1+\sqrt{5})^1 = 1+\sqrt{5}$ **[1]**

2nd term: $(1+\sqrt{5})^2 = (1 + \sqrt{5})(1 + \sqrt{5}) = 1 + \sqrt{5} + \sqrt{5} + 5$

$= 6 + 2\sqrt{5}$ **[1]**

3rd term: $(6 + 2\sqrt{5})(1 + \sqrt{5}) = 6 + 6\sqrt{5} + 2\sqrt{5} + 2 \times 5$

$= 16 + 8\sqrt{5}$ **[1]**

21. $y = x^2 - 6x + 11$

$y = (x - 3)^2 - 9 + 11$ **[1]**

$y = (x - 3)^2 + 2$ **[1]**

Turning point is (3, 2) **[1]**

By completing the square to get $y = (x - a)^2 + b$, we know the turning point is (a, b).

22. $BD^2 = 10.8^2 + 12.3^2 - 2 \times 10.8 \times 12.3 \times \cos 52$ **[1]**

$BD^2 = 267.93 - 265.68 \cos 52$

$BD = \sqrt{104.3610592}$

$BD = 10.21572607 \text{ cm}$ **[1]**

$\frac{\sin(BDC)}{12.3} = \frac{\sin 52}{10.21572607}$ **[1]**

$\sin(BDC) = \frac{\sin 52 \times 12.3}{10.21572607}$

$\sin(BDC) = 0.9487854513$

Angle $BDC = \sin^{-1}(0.9487854513) = 71.5835...°$ **[1]**
Angle $ADB = 180° - 71.5935...° = 108.4065...°$
Angle $BAD = 180° - 29° - 108.4065...° = 42.6°$ **[1]**

> Use the cosine rule to find BD, then use the sine rule to find angle BDC.

PRACTICE EXAM 2

Paper 1 (pages 41–52)

1. **(a)** 0.0042   **(b)** 350×0.88 **(c)** $14\,400\,\text{cm}^2$
2. **(a)** $2x = 15$
   $x = 7.5$
   (b) $2x^2 + 8x - 3x - 12$ **[1]**
   $2x^2 + 5x - 12$ **[1]**

   > You will get the first mark for all terms correct, with one error in the symbols.

   (c) $ab(a - 1)$ **[2]**
   [1 mark for an incomplete factorisation:
   $a(ab - b)$ **or** $b(a^2 - a)$**]**
3.

200	30	6		
4000	600	120	**20**	
1400	210	42	**7**	

   [1]

   $236 \times 27 = 6372$ **[1]**
   63.72 **[1]**
4. $5x - 20 = 3x - 15$ **[1]**
   $2x = 5$
   $x = 2.5$ **[1]**
5. **(a)** $3 \div 11 = 0.272727...$ **[1]**
   $0.\dot{2}\dot{7}$ **[1]**

   > Use a long division method, e.g. bus stop.

   (b) $\frac{3}{5} \times \frac{15}{4}$ **[1]** $= \frac{45}{20}$ **[1]** $= 2\frac{5}{20} = 2\frac{1}{4}$ **[1]**
6. **(a)** $\frac{8}{30}$ or $\frac{4}{15}$
   (b) $\frac{3}{30} \times \frac{5}{30}$ **[1]** $= \frac{1}{10} \times \frac{1}{6} = \frac{1}{60}$ **[1]**

   > Use the AND rule.

7. $\frac{350 - 280}{350}$ **[1]** $= \frac{70}{350} = \frac{1}{5} = 20\%$ **[1]**
8. **(a)**

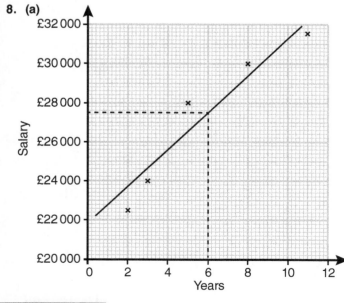

[2 marks for all five points correctly plotted; 1 mark for one error only]
   (b) Answer in range £27 000 to £28 000
   (c) It is outside the given range of the data.
9. $\frac{100}{600} = \frac{1}{6}$, $\frac{1}{6} \times 30000 = 5000$ people may require a tent **[1]**
   Assume all 5000 will be sleeping in a tent; assume 4 people share a tent or assume 2 people share a tent. **[1]**
   $5000 \div 4 = 1250$ tents or $5000 \div 2 = 2500$ tents **[1]**
10. **(a)** Reflection **[1]** in the line $y = x$ **[1]**
    (b)

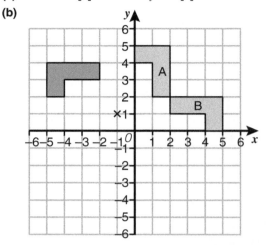

[2 marks if fully correct; 1 mark for correct orientation]
11. $51 = \frac{\text{distance}}{0.666...}$ **[1]**
    $d = 51 \times 0.666... = 34$ miles **[1]** from Manchester to Knutsford services
    $66 - 34 = 32$ miles from Knutsford services to Stoke-on-Trent
    Speed $= \frac{32}{0.5} = 64$ mph **[1]**

    > Use the formula speed $= \frac{\text{distance}}{\text{time}}$, converting minutes into hours.

12. Triangle ABC is congruent to triangle GHI. **[1]**
    Using ASA both triangles have a 5 cm side between the angles of 30° and 70°, proving that all three sides are identical. **[1]**

    > In triangle ABC, use the angle fact that angles in a triangle add up to 180°.

13. Arc length $= \frac{2 \times \pi \times 2x}{4}$ **[1]** $= x\pi$
    Perimeter $= x\pi + 2x + 2x$
    $= 4x + x\pi$ or $x(4 + \pi)$ **[1 mark for either]**

    > Use the formula: Circumference $= 2\pi r$

14. £16 000 = 80% **[1]**
    £2000 = 10%
    £20 000 = 100%
    No, with correct working seen **[1]**
15. $-2 + 2 \times r = 4$
    $q + 2 \times 8 = 21$ **[1]**
    $q = 5$ and $r = 3$ **[1]**
16. **(a)** $(4x \pm 13)(4x \pm 13)$ **[1]**
    $(4x + 13)(4x - 13)$ **[1]**
    (b) $(x - 12)(x + 3) = 0$ **[1]**
    $x - 12 = 0$ or $x + 3 = 0$
    $x = 12$ and $x = -3$ **[1]**

17. $877.5 \leqslant m < 882.5$

[1 mark for correct numbers; 1 mark for correct symbols]

> Error interval is half of 5 miles above and below 880 miles.

18. Using $y = mx + c$, $m = -\frac{1}{3}$ **[1]**

$y = -\frac{1}{3}x + c$

$0 = -\frac{1}{3} \times 4 + c$ **[1]**

$c = \frac{4}{3}$

$y = -\frac{1}{3}x + \frac{4}{3}$ or $3y = 4 - x$ **[1 mark for either]**

> The gradient perpendicular to m is $-\frac{1}{m}$

19.

Sequence	3		11		23		39		59		83
First difference		8		12		16		20		24	
Second difference			4		4		4		4		

[1 mark for finding the second difference is 4]

The nth term for the sequence must be in the form

$an^2 + bn + c$

When $n = 1$: $a + b + c = 3$ (Equation 1)

When $n = 2$: $4a + 2b + c = 11$ (Equation 2)

When $n = 3$: $9a + 3b + c = 23$ (Equation 3)

Equation 3 – Equation 2: $5a + b = 12$ (Equation 4)

Equation 2 – Equation 1: $3a + b = 8$ (Equation 5)

Equation 4 – Equation 5: $2a = 4$, $a = 2$

Substitute $a = 2$ into Equation 4.

$10 + b = 12$, $b = 2$

Substitute $a = 2$ and $b = 2$ into Equation 1.

$2 + 2 + c = 3$, $c = -1$ **[1 mark for finding a, b or c]**

$2n^2 + 2n - 1$ is the nth term for the sequence **[1]**

100th term $= 2(100)^2 + 2(100) - 1 = 20\,199$ **[1]**

20. $2500 \div 2000 \; (= 1.25)$ **[1]**

$(\sqrt[3]{1.25})^2 = (1.16...)$ **[1]**

$1250 \div 1.16... $ **[1]**

1077 m^2 **[1]**

> Find the area scale factor by cube rooting and then squaring the volume scale factor.

21. $(x + 1)(x - 6) \leqslant 0$ **[1]**

$x + 1 \geqslant 0$ and $x - 6 \leqslant 0$ **[1]**

$-1 \leqslant x \leqslant 6$ **[1]**

$x = -1, 0, 1, 2, 3, 4, 5$ or 6 **[1]**

> Substitute the integers into the original inequality to check that they work.

22. $AC = \sqrt{3^2 + 3^2}$ **[1]** $= \sqrt{18}$

$AM = \frac{\sqrt{18}}{2}$, where M is the midpoint of AC.

Height $= EM = \sqrt{5^2 - \left(\frac{\sqrt{18}}{2}\right)^2}$ **[1]**

$EM = \sqrt{5^2 - \frac{18}{4}}$ **[1]**

$EM = \sqrt{25 - 4.5} = \sqrt{20.5}$

$a = 20.5$ **[1]**

> Use Pythagoras' theorem twice.

23. $\frac{7}{3x} \times \frac{6x}{x - 1}$ **[1]**

$\frac{42x}{3x(x - 1)}$ **[1]**

$\frac{14}{x - 1}$ **[1]**

> Use the AND rule.

24. (a) Missing number in circle: $28 - (8 + 2 + 5) = 13$

Missing number outside circles:

$50 - (13 + 8 + 2 + 5 + 8 + 3 + 9) = 2$

(b) $\frac{8 + 2}{8 + 2 + 3 + 9} = \frac{10}{22}$ or $\frac{5}{11}$

(c) $\frac{2}{5 + 2 + 3 + 8} = \frac{2}{18}$ or $\frac{1}{9}$

25. $\left(\frac{\sqrt{3} + 1}{4}\right)^{-1} = \frac{4}{\sqrt{3} + 1}$ **[1]**

$\frac{4}{\sqrt{3} + 1} \times \frac{\sqrt{3} - 1}{\sqrt{3} - 1}$ **[1]**

$\frac{4\sqrt{3} - 4}{(\sqrt{3} + 1)(\sqrt{3} - 1)} = \frac{4\sqrt{3} - 4}{3 - \sqrt{3} + \sqrt{3} - 1}$ **[1]**

$\frac{4\sqrt{3} - 4}{2} = 2\sqrt{3} - 2$ **[1]**

> Find the reciprocal of the original fraction and then rationalise the denominator.

Paper 2 (pages 53–65)

1. (a) $\frac{3 - (-4)}{(-4)^2} = \frac{7}{16}$

(b) $2a - a - 3b - 2b = a - 5b$

2. $\frac{1\,587\,392 - 1\,372\,658}{1\,372\,658} = \frac{214\,734}{1\,372\,658} \times 100$ **[1]**

15.6% **[1]**

3. $2 \div (15 - 11) = 0.5$ **[1]** sweets per share

15×0.5 **[1]** $= 7\frac{1}{2}$ sweets **[1]**

4. $0.6 \times 162 = 108$ **[1]** going to a theme park

$\frac{8}{27} \times 162 = 48$ **[1]** going ice-skating

Staying in school: $162 - 108 - 48$ **[1]** $= 6$ **[1]** students

5. (a) $2, 7, 12, 17, 22$

(b) $5n$ **[1]** $5n - 3$ **[1]**

> Find the difference (going up in fives means $5n$).

(c) When $n = 27$: $5 \times (27) - 3 = 132$

6. One interior angle $= \frac{(10 - 2) \times 180}{10}$ **[1]** $= 144°$ **[1]**

OR Exterior angle $= 360° \div 10 = 36°$ **[1]**.

Interior angle $= 180° - 36° = 144°$ **[1]**

Area of sector $= \frac{144°}{360°} \times (\pi \times 5^2)$ **[1]** $= 10\pi \text{ cm}^2$ **[1]**

> You will need to know that the sum of angles inside an n-sided polygon add up to $(n - 2) \times 180°$. You will also need to know the formula: Area of sector $= \frac{\text{Angle of sector}}{360°} \times (\pi r^2)$

7. (a) 8 chefs: 140 guests

1 chef: 17.5 guests **[1]**

10 chefs: 175 guests

10 chefs **[1]**

> Divide by 8 to find out how many guests one chef can prepare for.

(b) One of the following assumptions:

The same amount of food is prepared for both meals.

Each chef works at the same rate.

There is the same amount of time to prepare the food for both meals.

8. Volume of ice cubes: $16 \times 2 \times 2 \times 2 = 128\,cm^3$ **[1]**

Volume of cylinder: $\pi \times 6^2 \times h$ **[1]**

$36\pi h = 128$ **[1]**

$h = \frac{128}{36\pi} = 1.13\,cm$ **[1]**

9. (a) $(9, -4)$ **[1 mark for each correct value]**

> Plus 2 in the x-direction, subtract 5 in the y-direction.

(b) For $y = mx + c$, gradient $m = \frac{\text{change in } y}{\text{change in } x} = \frac{-4-1}{9-7} = \frac{-5}{2}$ **[1]**

Substitute $(7, 1)$ into the equation:

$y = \left(\frac{-5}{2}\right)x + c$

$1 = \left(\frac{-5}{2}\right) \times 7 + c$ **[1]**

$c = 1 + \left(\frac{35}{2}\right) = 18.5$

Equation of the line:

$y = \left(\frac{-5}{2}\right)x + 18.5$ or $2y = -5x + 37$ **[1]**

10. (a) £632 000 000 − £12 500 000 = £619 500 000 **[1]**

£6.195 × 10^8 **[1]**

(b) (£6.195 × 10^8) × (2.1 × 10^{-3}) **[1]** = £1 300 950 **[1]**

> Divide 2.1×10^{-1}% by 100 to find the equivalent decimal 2.1×10^{-3}

11. (a)

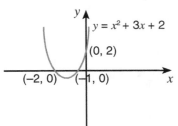

[2 marks if fully correct; 1 mark if graph intercepts positive y-axis once; 1 mark if the graph intercepts negative x-axis twice]

> When $x = 0$, $y = (0)^2 + 3(0) + 2 = 2$, giving the y-intercept as $(0, 2)$. Solve the equation $x^2 + 3x + 2 = 0$ by factorising, $(x + 1)(x + 2) = 0$, giving the x-intercepts as $(-2, 0)$ and $(-1, 0)$.

(b) When $x = -1.5$: $y = (-1.5)^2 + 3(-1.5) + 2 = -0.25$

Turning point $(-1.5, -0.25)$

> Alternatively, complete the square to get:
> $y = (x + 1.5)^2 - 0.25$

12. $\cos 62° = \frac{\text{adjacent}}{658}$ **[1]**

Adjacent = $658 \times \cos 62°$ **[1]** = 308.91 m **[1]**

> The angle of elevation from the boat to the man is 62° since alternate angles are equal.

13. (a) $\frac{6^{7-2}}{6^6} = \frac{6^5}{6^6}$ **[1]** $= 6^{-1} = \frac{1}{6}$ **[1]**

(b) $(2^3)^x = 2^4$ **[1]**

$3x = 4$

$x = \frac{4}{3}$ **[1]**

> Change 8 and 16 so that they have the same base number, 2.

14. $x = 0.136363636\ldots$

$10x = 1.363636363\ldots$

$1000x = 136.363636\ldots$ **[1 mark for any one of these]**

$990x = 135$ **[1]**

$x = \frac{135}{990}$ **[1]** $= \frac{3}{22}$

15. (a) Elliot or Wiki with a correct reason:

Elliot has the largest interquartile range or Wiki has the largest range.

(b) One correct statement **[1]** with correct value **[1]**:

Natasha and Wiki have the same median (5 mins), Niall and Natasha have the same range (6.5 mins) or Niall and Wiki have the same interquartile range (4 mins).

16. $x(5x - 4) = 2$ **[1]**

$5x^2 - 4x - 2 = 0$ **[1]**

$\frac{-(-4)\pm\sqrt{(-4)^2 - 4 \times 5 \times -2}}{2 \times 5}$ **[1]**

$\frac{4\pm\sqrt{16 + 40}}{10} = \frac{4\pm\sqrt{56}}{10}$ **[1]**

$x = 1.15$ and $x = -0.35$ **[1]**

> Use the quadratic formula $\frac{-b\pm\sqrt{b^2 - 4ac}}{2a}$, when $ax^2 + bx + c = 0$

17. (a) Tangent drawn at 4 seconds **[1]**

Acceleration = $\frac{-2}{2}$ **[1]** = $-1\,m/s^2$ **[1] (accept −0.8 to −1.2)**

> Calculate the gradient of the tangent drawn at 4 s.

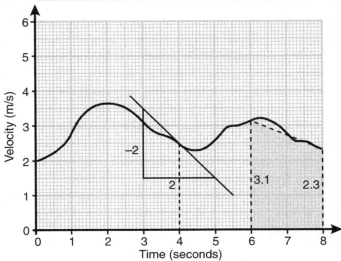

(b) $\left(\frac{3.1 + 2.3}{2}\right) \times 2$ **[1]** = 5.4 m **[1] (accept 5.2 to 5.6)**

> Estimate the area under the graph between 6 and 8 s by using the formula for the area of a trapezium.

18. (a)

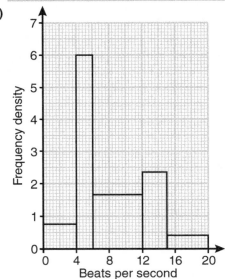

Beats per second	$0 < b \leq 4$	$4 < b \leq 6$	$6 < b \leq 12$	$12 < b \leq 15$	$15 < b \leq 20$
Frequency	3	12	10	7	2

[2 marks for fully correct graph and frequencies; 1 mark for correct attempt to find the height of the last bar]

Find the frequency density by dividing the frequency by the class width: $2 \div 5 = 0.4$, $7 \div 3 = 2.\dot{3}$, $10 \div 6 = 1.\dot{6}$. Label the frequency density axis and find the height of all of the bars. Find the area of the bars to find the missing frequencies.

(b) $\frac{3 + 12 + 10 + 7 + 2}{2} = \frac{34}{2} = 17$ **[1]** qualified

$6 + 1.2 = 7.2$ **[1]** beats per minute

The 17th person is three squares into the third bar since $2 \div 1.\dot{6} = 1.2$

19. $\frac{1}{2} \times 5 \times 8 \times \sin x = 10.15$ **[1]**

$x = \sin^{-1}(0.5075)$ **[1]**

$x = 30.5°$ **[1]**

Use the formula: Area of triangle $= \frac{1}{2} ab \sin C$.

20. $y = 18 - 2x$

$3x^2 + (18 - 2x)^2 = 139$ **[1]**

$3x^2 + 324 - 36x - 36x + 4x^2 = 139$ **[1]**

$7x^2 - 72x + 185 = 0$

$(7x - 37)(x - 5) = 0$ **[1]**

$x = \frac{37}{7}$ or $5\frac{2}{7}$ **[1]**

$y = 18 - 2 \times \frac{37}{7}$

$y = 7\frac{3}{7}$ **[1]**

Substitute the second equation into the first. Expand, simplify, rearrange and then factorise to solve the quadratic equation. Substitute x back into one of the original equations to find y.

21. ε

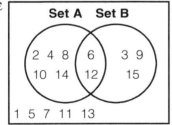

[3 marks if fully correct; deduct 1 mark for each error or omission]

Even numbers in Set A. Multiples of 3 in Set B. Even multiples of 3 in the overlap. Any other numbers in the universal set go outside the circles.

22. P(three girls being picked)

$= \frac{13}{25} \times \frac{12}{24} \times \frac{11}{23}$ **[1]** $= \frac{1716}{13800}$ **[1]** $= \frac{143}{1150}$

P(at least one boy being picked) = 1 − P(three girls being picked)

$1 - \frac{143}{1150}$ **[1]** $= \frac{1007}{1150}$ **[1]**

You may find it useful to draw a tree diagram to show all eight possible outcomes.

Paper 3 (pages 66–78)

1. (a) False: a negative number cubed gives a negative answer, e.g. $-2^3 = -8$

(b) True: a negative or a positive number squared gives a positive answer, e.g. $(-2)^2 = 2^2 = 4$

(c) False: when $x = 2$, 2^2 is equal to 2×2.

2. (a) $-3 \leq 2x < 6$ **[1]**

$-1.5 \leq x < 3$ **[1]**

Add 3 to each part, then divide by 2.

(b) $-1, 0, 1, 2$

3. (a) Discrete **[1]**

Primary **[1]**

(b) Each student is equally likely to be picked **[1]**

4. (a) B   **(b)** A

5. (a) $\frac{38}{203}$ of $48752 \approx \frac{40}{200} \times 50000$ **[1]** $= 10000$ **[1]**

Round each number to 1 significant figure.

(b) An over-estimate since $\frac{40}{200} > \frac{38}{203}$ and $50000 > 48752$ **[1]**

Assumption: A similar proportion of students from every school in England will not bring a calculator to the exam. **[1]**

6. Premium bonds: £15 × 2.5 × 3 **[1]** = £112.50 **[1]**

Local bank: £2500 × 1.01 × 1.015 × 1.02 **[1]** = £2614.13 **[1]**

Local bank is likely to give the best investment **[1]**

7. $180 - 8x = 32°$ **[1]**

$x = 18.5°$ **[1]**

Angle $ABC = 180 - 6x$

Angle $ABC = 180 - 6(18.5°)$ **[1]**

Angle $ABC = 69°$ **[1]**

Use the fact that there are two isosceles triangles which each add up to 180°.

8. (a) $18x + 8x + 11x + 3x = 1$ **[1]**

$40x = 1$

$x = 0.025$ **[1]**

$0.025 \times 11 = 0.275 = 27.5\%$ **[1]**

(b) $3(0.025) \times 80$ **[1]** = 6 people **[1]**

Multiply the probability for vegetarian by 80 people.

9. (a) $\frac{10 \text{ km}}{1.6}$ **[1]** 6.25 miles **[1]**

6.25×133 **[1]** $= 831.25$ calories **[1]**

To convert miles into kilometres, you must know that 1 mile = 1.6 km

(b) Speed $= \frac{6.25}{1.25}$ **[1]** = 5 mph **[1]**

Answer should be B or D. Since his speed (5 mph) is much slower than his usual average speed, he must be running on difficult terrain. **[1]**

1 hour 15 minutes converts to 1.25 hours. Then use the formula: Speed $= \frac{\text{Distance}}{\text{Time}}$

10. Volume of sphere $= \frac{4}{3}\pi(5)^3$ **[1]** $= 523.598...$ mm³ **[1]**

523.598... $\div (3 + 5)$ **[1]** $= 65.449...$ mm³ per share.

Volume of mint crème filling $= 65.449... \times 5 = 327.2$ mm³ **[1]**

> Share the total volume of the sphere in the ratio 3 : 5

11. $AD = AB$ (adjacent sides in a kite are equal)

AM is a shared line in both triangles.

$DM = MB$ since M is the midpoint of DB

[2 marks for all three statements; 1 mark for at least two statements]

Therefore, using SSS, triangle AMD is congruent to triangle AMB. **[1]**

12. $a \times 6 - 6 = b$ **[1]**

Equation 1: $6a - b = 6$

Equation 2: $4a - b = 3$

Equation 1 – Equation 2: $2a = 3$ **[1]**

$a = 1.5$

Substitute $a = 1.5$ into Equation 1

$6 \times 1.5 - b = 6$ **[1]**

$a = 1.5, b = 3$ **[1]**

> Solve the two equations simultaneously.

13. (R, R), (R, P), **(R, S)**

(P, R), (P, P), (P, S)

(S, R), **(S, P)**, (S, S)

P (win) $= \frac{3}{9}$ **[1]**

P (Joel wins first two) $= \frac{3}{9} \times \frac{3}{9}$ **[1]** $= \frac{9}{81}$ or $\frac{1}{9}$ **[1]**

> List all the possible outcomes for the game. Then use the **AND** rule for the probability that Joel wins the first **AND** the second.

14. $\left(x + \frac{b}{2}\right)^2 - \left(\frac{b}{2}\right)^2 + c$ **[1]**

$D = \frac{b}{2}$ **[1]** $E = c - \frac{b^2}{4}$ **[1]**

> Use the method of completing the square.

15. (a) $\frac{26}{46} \times 100$ **[1]** $= 56.5\%$ (to 1 d.p.) **[1]**

> Identify 26 from the graph by drawing a vertical line at 15 m.

(b) $46 - 36$ **[1]** $= 10$ rides **[1]**

> Identify 36 from the graph by drawing a vertical line at 20 m.

16. $POR = 180° - 2x$ **[1]**

$PQR = 90° - x$ **[1]**

Reason: Angle at the centre is twice the angle at the circumference. Triangle POR is isosceles. **[1]**

17. (a) $y = x^2 - 2$

$x = \sqrt{y + 2}$ **[1]**

$f^{-1}(x) = \sqrt{x + 2}$ **[1]** **[Accept $\pm\sqrt{x + 2}$]**

> Rearrange f(x) to make x the subject.

(b) $fg(x) = (5 - 3x)^2 - 2$

$fg(5) = (5 - 3 \times 5)^2 - 2$ **[1]**

$fg(5) = (-10)^2 - 2$

$fg(5) = 98$ **[1]**

> Substitute the function g(x) into the function f(x).

18. $x^2 + x^2 = 40^2$ **[1]**

$2x^2 = 40^2 = 1600$

$x^2 = 800$

$x = \sqrt{800}$ **[1]**

$x = \sqrt{(16 \times 25 \times 2)} = \sqrt{16} \times \sqrt{25} \times \sqrt{2} = 4 \times 5 \times \sqrt{2} = 20\sqrt{2}$ **[1]**

$a = 20$ and $b = 2$ **[1]**

> Make a sketch of the triangle. Use Pythagoras' theorem to find x.

19. $l \propto s^2$

$l = ks^2$ **[1]**

$2000 = k \times 240^2$

$k = \frac{2000}{240^2} = 0.03472\dot{2}$ **[1]**

$l = 0.03472\dot{2}s^2$

$2400 = 0.03472\dot{2} \times s^2$ **[1]**

$s^2 = \frac{2400}{0.03472}$

$s = \sqrt{\frac{2400}{0.03472}} = 263$ kph **[1]**

20. (a) Curve must pass through the origin (0,0)

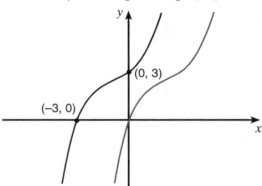

> The curve has been translated three squares to the right.

(b) (0, 0) **[1]** and (3, 3) **[1]**

21.

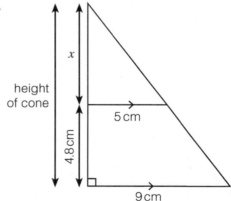

Scale factor: $9 \div 5 = 1.8$ **[1]**

$x \times 1.8 = x + 4.8$ **[1]**

$0.8x = 4.8$

$x = 6$ cm **[1]**

Height of cone $= 6 + 4.8$ **[1]** $= 10.8$ cm **[1]**

> Draw similar triangles to represent the height of the original cone.